Patterns

PATTERNS

Ronald Harvey

GANESHA PUBLISHING

EDITION SYNAPSE

Published in 2001 by

Ganesha Publishing Ltd
PO Box 27760
London E5 8UU, United Kingdom
www.ganesha-publishing.com

Patterns
ISBN 1-86210-025-X

British Library Cataloguing-in-Publication Data
A CIP record of this title is available from the British Library

Printed in England by T J International, Padstow, UK

To Erica for her help and encouragement, and to Andrew Dewhurst, without whom what follows might never have been published.

What pattern connects the crab to the lobster and the orchid to the primrose and all four of them to me? And me to you?

Gregory Bateson

... the drift of all the evidence we have seems to me to sweep us very strongly toward the belief in some form of superhuman life with which we may, unknown to ourselves, be coconscious. We may be in the universe as dogs and cats are in our libraries, seeing the books and hearing the conversation, but having no inkling of the meaning of it all.

William James, *A Pluralistic Universe*

Contents

Preface

What follows probably needs some preliminary explanation. Basically it is an attempt to make sense of a world which, to many, must seem increasingly, almost terrifyingly, senseless. Certainly it must appear so to the Third World even if the West has, on the face of it, come to terms with it. In trying to find a way through the morass I seem to have come up with a rag-bag of ideas with apparently little coherence or rational sequence. Matters which have ostensibly little connection with each other are often juxtaposed. This is partly planned and partly random. Rational structure is confronted by irrational function, the chaotic, even the absurd. Paul Valéry claimed that chaos was a condition of the mind's fertility. The rational mind is tightly controlled and leaves little room for the unexpected or the radically new. It is the subconscious mind which is more often the fertile soil for the 'Eureka' experience, as a plethora of literature on the subject has amply demonstrated. Compost heaps are fertile breeding grounds. If the reader finds the dung-heap placed next to the laboratory this may be as often due to design as to chance.

The whole history of invention and discovery is witness to the fact that one has to go beyond logic to intuition, paradox and the irrational, that convention must be broken, the rules disobeyed, if one is to break new ground. Most of us obey the rules and defend them jealously. Those disturbed in mind are unaware of them or ignore them. Genius surpasses them or shatters them, but in turn sets up new ones which again in their turn have to be broken. Belief and disbelief, order and chaos, structure and function are made use of here as backgrounds to the assessment of experience. Finally the haphazard arrangement is meant to hint at the interconnectedness of things, even the most unlikely. After all, the most unlikely are often the most fruitful.

This is not a book for the specialist or expert but rather for the intelligent average man or woman, a book connecting different fields of experience rather exploring each in depth. My sole recommendation to those rash enough to read what I have written is to heed the warning 'periculosum est credere' and then disregard it. Live dangerously in the mind, if not in the body. The mind, unlike the brain, is not caged in the cranium. It is open to the world and should be kept open. There is much to discover.

When the idea of this book first came into my mind I had not yet read *Order out of Chaos* by Ilya Prigogin and his colleague Isabelle Stengers. I was delighted to find myself in agreement with the general tenor of their book. I have not been able to follow all the more recondite science or mathematics but the general idea I seem to have picked up through some sort of affinitive telepathy. The ideas of determinism, chance, free-will and their apparent irreconcilability have always interested me and in *Order out of Chaos* there seemed to be a way of fitting them together.

Venturing into problematical territory I have attempted to relate philosophical and scientific beliefs to human and social behaviour. I have also touched on philosophies of history by such writers as Vico, Hegel and Marx. The exploration of relationships thrown up by such geometrical structures as Ernst Cassirer's 'Symbolic Forms' and Plato's 'Elements' in philosophy, science, politics and social orientation is also, I suggest, a subject worth enquiry. Such structures influence our lives and frame our experience more than we think. This is an excursion largely into the blue. The limits of enquiry have been well trodden by the gamekeepers and wardens of what is permissible to ramblers. This book is about ideas, some probably impermissible. Even error can be fruitful and facts, as we have now reluctantly come to realise, are too often fiction.

A major theme I have tried to pursue is the interconnectedness of everything. Reductionism and the urge to examine everything in watertight compartments has been, in my view, a restrictive contribution to thought. The gamekeepers have been too obtrusive and restrictive. This book is a manual for trespass.

Finally I would like to suggest that everything, absolutely everything, rests on belief. Nothing is known absolutely, and, short of perfection, cannot be. As Karl Popper put it: 'certainty is a chimera ... . If you insist on strict proof in the empirical sciences, you will never learn from experience, and never learn from it how wrong you are.' And again from Popper: 'every scientific statement must remain tentative for ever.'

So we are back with belief, but that of course is beset with snags. 'Periculosum est credere.' Indeed it is, but then danger is the spice of life, and without belief there is no life.

Foreword

The main subject of this book is structure, the patterning of life, whether the pattern is natural or man-made, physical or mental, anatomical or physiological. Structures are, of course, related to functions and they act on each other reciprocally. The late biologist and cyberneticist Ludwig von Bertalanffy described structure as a form of slowed-down, compacted function, and function as a speeded-up, fluid version of structure. A thigh bone, which we would regard as a structure, is not a static, unchangeable part of the human body. It is in slow, but continual, movement. It grows rapidly in childhood, slows, hardens, becomes brittle and porous in old age. Over the years its shape is altered by the pull of the muscles which move it and by the weight it has to bear. Its use, its function determines, to a greater extent than one would imagine, its basic structure.

Similarly with function. The function of the thigh bone besides that of weight bearing is exercise, walking or running. Such exercise is to some extent determined by the structure. It is limited but highly flexible in the child's thigh, most free and strong in that of the young athlete, most restricted and slowed down in the aged or infirm. Anatomy tends to determine physiology while at the same time physiology helps to shape anatomy.

This ubiquitous pair, structure and function, which are also particular and patterned instances of matter and energy, provide us with co-ordinates with which we can orientate ourselves in our world for they are also related respectively with space and time. They are present in the mind as much as in the body. They penetrate, infiltrate, confine and set free every aspect of human life. There are structures of parts and equally of wholes, structures of periods and periods of structure. Structures may coalesce into patterns or separate into parts. Mentally they may serve us as blueprints for this or that, frames of reference, compasses, landmarks or maps with which to find where we are or to see our way forward, or even to tell us the time, for structures like watches may help us to measure time as well as space.

Let us take as a spatial, structural example, a human arm and hand, while at the same time we consider its temporal, functional aspect, say the movement of grasping (active) and on the other hand the sensation of feeling or touch (passive). The structure here is not just the arrangement of bone, muscle and skin; it consists also of the nerve pathways which carry the messages for action or sensation. There are efferent motor nerves conveying messages from the brain to the muscles of the hand, and afferent sensory nerves conveying messages from skin surfaces back to the brain. The structure here is the nerve complex, the function the messages – whether motor or sensory – resulting in action or sensation. The function cannot take place without the structure which it uses. The structure is meaningless without the function which it canalises and for which it affords a pathway. Cut a motor nerve and the relevant muscle will not work. Cut a sensory nerve and the result is loss of feeling.

Everything we do in life and everything that happens to us can be related to some sort of structure, either physical or mental. Sometimes the relationship is negative. We may reject or revolt against a particular structure yet we cannot avoid its influence entirely, for rejection itself demonstrates the importance of structure; the denial is the necessary other face of assertion. One is contained within the other. The chapter I have included on Simone Weil vividly demonstrates a revolt against orthodox structure as a consequence of which she managed to construct her own, paradoxical though it may seem to many. Natural, as opposed to geometrical, structures are not rigid but flexible, bending with the flow of function. There is always room in a general structure for individual variation.

What follows is not meant to be taken at the foot of the letter, but rather as a springboard for the imagination. Its 'facts' are disputable, as indeed all so-called facts should be. Many facts are fictions dressed up in acceptable clothes and we prefer them that way. We can't help it. We live by fictions. The Latin 'fictio' is a noun of which the verb 'fingere' means to make, to invent, to conceive, to form. Isaac Newton in a rash moment exclaimed 'Hypotheses non fingo', one of the most transparent lies in history. We are 'fingering' all the time. Our world is a fiction which we nevertheless are programmed to see as fact. We conceive it, invent it, make it ourselves and then pretend we don't. We like to think it is purely the result of external cause and effect, of God, of Nature, of science, of fate, of determinism, of chance or anything else when all the time the 'deus ex machina' is ourselves. Our world is a fiction, a world of appearances, of phenomena, as Plato, Kant and Prospero in *The Tempest*, and many others have been trying to tell us for centuries. Now relativity and quantum physics have almost put an end to the materialism which was foisted on the fiction and which we still cling to since there seemed nothing else. Without matter where were we? It now appears we are not even skating on thin ice since the ice itself has melted. Matter was just a form of energy and both were appearances. As a consequence it is with appearances that we have to deal, for – since we are as we are – this is all we can do.

Frameworks

When we attempt to think rationally it helps to have a basic structure which may serve as a framework for the orientation, location and development of ideas. Such a structure could provide us with signposts or benchmarks to which we may resort when lost, or a firm base from which to venture into the unknown. Such a need has, indeed, been recognised for at least two millennia. Perhaps the most well-known and basic of such structures is the intersection of the earth's two 'great circles', the meridian and horizon. The meridian and horizon are not, of course, 'things'. We cannot touch them or move them even if we imagine we can see them. They are mental projections. We can mark their derivatives on our map or globe of the earth as lines of longitude and latitude, and if we do they help us to read the map, providing us with co-ordinates or reference points. In his book, *The Philosophy of Symbolic Forms*, the philosopher Ernst Cassirer pointed out that the intersection of these two 'great circles' when considered two-dimensionally as a meridian–horizon cross, had formed for centuries a basic framework of co-ordinates for mental and physical advancement in many fields. The Romans notably made use of them. Italian cities, the layout of Roman camps in which the two main thoroughfares, the Decumanus and the Cardo, related to the meridian and horizon while these two diameters also influenced the ground plan of the Roman house. Temples and cathedrals were also similarly orientated. Even the law and theoretical science were permeated by such basic co-ordinates.

Does geometrical structure really have an influence on the way we think? Both the Pythagorean physician Alcmaeon of Croton and the astronomer Johannes Kepler seemed to think so. Alcmaeon, who preceded that other father of medicine, Hippocrates, by a generation, looked on it from the point of view of disease, Kepler from that of astronomy.

Both had the idea that the mind related to a clock-like structure of twelve, whether hours, months, seasons or purely abstract divisions – a division in which the cardinal points were indicated by the revolution of the earth on itself, representing Midday/Midnight, Sunrise/Sunset, and the revolution of the earth round the sun representing Midsummer/Midwinter, Spring Equinox/Autumn Equinox. The Chinese, like Alcmaeon, also related it to disease. In Chinese acupuncture there are twelve meridians and twelve pulses. Moreover, its technique depends to some extent on the hour, in the twelve-hour day or night.

This $3 \times 4 = 12$ motif turns up in the most unlikely situations. It occurs, consciously or unconsciously, in Immanuel Kant's *Critique of Pure Reason,* where his twelve famous 'categories' were again divided into four threes like the four seasons, and these were, of course, entirely abstract 'a priori' conditions at the base of all human conjecture. It occurs again in genetics, where DNA, the genetic code, consists of four bases – Adenine, Thymine, Guanine and Cytosine. From these four bases sixty-four nucleotide triplets arise (four to the power of three, $4 \times 4 \times 4 = 64$). In Aristotle's logic a syllogism has three propositions and there are four main kinds of syllogism. Then there are the four elements and three 'gunas' (rajas, tamas and sattva) of Indian philosophy. The medieval university or 'studium generale' divided its faculties into the 'Trivium' and 'Quadrivium'. Again Aristotle divided movement into three sorts – qualitative change, quantitative change and motion from place to place. The simplest perfect solid is the tetrahedron, in which the four sides are composed of triangles. The most perfect solid is the dodecahedron, a twelve-sided figure.

The number four haunts us. We note it in the four dimensions of the space–time continuum, in the four forces of nature (nuclear, electromagnetic, weak force (beta decay) and gravity). We come upon it again in embryology in the four-fold structure of the morula after the male gamete has fused with the female oocyte. Even Schopenhauer's *Fourfold Root of the Principle of Sufficient Reason* and Carl Jung's four 'psychic functions' are impaled on this four-fold structure reminiscent of our cardinal points of the compass and the meridian and horizon. One could think of countless other instances.

We can crucify the human body on this meridian–horizon cross. The upper pole of the meridian relates to the head, the lower pole to the feet. The right and left sides of the body are represented by the two poles of the horizontal axis. Unlike the poles of the meridian those of the horizon are mirror reflections of each other. Suppose we use such poles as pegs on which to hang concepts corresponding to the inherent logic of the structure. If we use the meridian to represent time, the horizon to stand for space, we immediately have a conceptual framework rich in potential for development. In his *Critique of Pure Reason* Kant regarded time as relating to interior sense, space to exterior sense, and if we accept this we can perhaps recognise that the meridian could relate to the mind, the horizon to the body and that the whole concept of inner and outer with all its ramifications could be ascribed to these two diameters respectively.

Other ideas fitting logically onto the general framework are heredity and environment. Heredity, since it is based on succession in time, must relate to the meridian. Environment, as extension in space, relates to the horizon. In Plato's *Republic* the meridian, as in mythology, was represented by the 'Spindle of Necessity'. It was the axis of the hub of the cosmos and was kept spinning by the three 'fates', Atropos, Clotho and Lachesis – Atropos singing of things to come, Clotho of the present and Lachesis of the past. Similarly in our meridian the arrow of time shoots upward from the seat of Lachesis at the lower pole to that of Atropos at the top, Clotho sitting midway between past and future astride the horizon. We could, indeed, label the lower pole 'Arche' or 'origins', the upper pole 'Telos' or 'ends', while the two poles of the horizon could be dubbed 'Voluntas' (will) and 'Arbitrium' (choice), each of which can only be exercised in the present. We now have a cross on which the vertical stands for Necessity, as in

Plato, the horizontal for Free-Will. It will be seen that if the vertical relates to Ends or Purpose then the horizontal stands for Means. We have been here, of course, dealing with incompatible levels of meaning. Each level should be interpreted separately. It is fundamentally misleading to conflate vertical meanings such as necessity, future, origins or ends. They have to be understood at different levels. Similarly with horizontal meanings. But within such levels it is obvious that necessity (vertical) is related to free-will (horizontal), that ends (vertical) relates to means (horizontal).

The logic of the framework is such that there is little danger of getting a particular concept hooked onto the wrong peg. It should be obvious that the meridian or vertical should stand for relationships in succession in time, or in depth, the horizontal for those that are co-eval, parallel, immediate or in breadth. Leaving time and space for a moment, let us look at the structure from the point of view of logic. Take Aristotle's four causes – formal cause, material cause, efficient cause and final cause. It stands to reason that the formal and final causes should occupy the lower and upper poles of the meridian respectively while the material and efficient causes, which relate to means rather than ends, should be allotted to the poles of the horizon.

In Cassirer's meridian–horizon structure music has its place on the vertical axis since it is extended in time. The plastic arts, painting and sculpture, have their place on the horizontal since they are extended in space. Their impression is immediate and instantaneous while that of music is protracted and sequential, involving duration of time. The means by which music is made, however, the instrument, piano, violin or whatever, and the pianist or violinist occupy the horizontal axis as means rather than ends. In Aristotelian terms the violin or piano is the 'material cause', the player is the 'efficient cause', while the music itself is both the 'formal' and the 'final cause'. Music, since it is related to time, can be considered as 'inner sense' (Kant) or mental, so it is fitting that it should occupy the vertical axis with which the mind is associated. The plastic arts involve matter, e.g., paint, wood, stone or whatever, and therefore relate to Kant's 'outer sense', or physical.

Music, according to Professor Michael Whiteman in his book *The Philosophy of Space and Time,* can be pegged on the framework in yet another way. He assigns music to the vertical axis but divides the vertical again into a vertical–horizontal cross in which the vertical represents a harmonic 'time-Gestalt', the horizontal a melodic 'time-Gestalt'. According to him there are Gestalten, or forms, combining both horizontal and vertical elements such as chord-progressions, tone contrast, tone quality and the development of contrapuntal ideas.

To illustrate an instance of the use of Cassirer's meridian and horizon cross, take now the multiple murder of schoolchildren in the United States in recent years, in various schools and all within a comparatively short period of time. The planning of the perpetrators is given form in the formal cause. Its final cause, the massacre, is, of course, the final cause. There is a time gap between the two indicated by the 'arrow of time' – one plans before one completes. On the poles of the horizon we find the material and the efficient causes. There is no time gap here since these poles relate to means not ends. The relationship is immediate. The material cause is the presence of fire-arms, the efficient cause those who press the trigger. Take away the two horizontal poles and there is no massacre. The guns and those who fire them are no longer there. Only the unaccomplished plan (the formal cause) and the final intention remain and without the means they are, of course, ineffective. The type of material cause may vary. It may be guns or fists and this may determine the final outcome. But since guns are lethal the outcome is likely to be lethal. The type of material cause helps to determine the final result regardless of the associations of the other three poles. Unfortunately in the United States the 'gun lobby' only too readily provides the material cause and the system of school bullying the efficient cause. Take away either one or the other and the potentiality for such a massacre vanishes.

The above framework may be used in a multitude of different fields to throw light on relationships and provide us with co-ordinates for rational thought. It does not, however, prescribe immutable laws but rather signposts for the orientation of concepts and how they may relate to each other. It also, by extrapolation, relates our thinking to the rotation of the earth on itself and to its revolution round the sun. This is, of course, a preposterous suggestion when set against modern orthodox belief. One wonders, indeed, if Cassirer himself fully recognised the enormity of his theory. But we are, one must repeat, not dealing with facts. It is all a priori, in the mind, though of ancient lineage going back over two thousand years to Plato's *Theaetetus*. 'Theories' as the French physiologist Claude Bernard has reminded us, 'are not true or false; they are fertile or sterile.' We have to try them out to find out which. Even if found to be fertile the structure is still no Procrustean bed. Ideas are not forced to fit it exactly but are broadly orientated and interrelated according to the signposting.

Other ideas which we may impale on the vertical–horizontal cross are those of superior and inferior rank or hierarchy which relate to the vertical contrasted with indifference to rank or egalitarianism, which belongs to the horizontal axis. Similarly, authoritarian or right-wing politics tend to the vertical; democratic, collective or socialist ideas relate more to the horizontal. The former, the vertical, represents domination or submission while the latter stands for relationships on equal terms.

Another such structure of equal or perhaps even greater significance is that introduced in Plato's *Timaeus* in the well-known framework of the four basic 'elements' – Fire, Air, Water and Earth. In the Renaissance there were other such structures. One was a twelve-fold division of a circle which was used as a mnemonic by such people as Giordano Bruno, but none had the staying power of Plato's elements, the combination of which contributed to the construction of the universe. It is, of course, a conceptual universe since the elements are not things but qualities. Plato goes out of his way to emphasise their immateriality. The Greek word for the elements was 'stoichea', which can also be translated as 'first principles'. These present us with four basic categories of meaning, a structure for the interpretation of the world. Taken more literally, the element Fire may represent the light of day, Air represents the wind and the atmosphere, Water the rain, rivers and seas, Earth the soil, rock and indeed the solid earth itself. Nothing can live or grow without the basic co-operation of the four elements. Seen as such they may be likened to 'particulars' but fundamentally they are 'universals' and as such have universal application.

Take psychology, for instance. The four elements have long been recognised as relating to temperament – Fire was fiery or choleric, Air was sanguine, Water was phlegmatic and Earth melancholic. This was a very primitive view of psychology but even now we can appreciate the elements' significance and the words choleric and melancholic still have meaning for us. Now take the case of forms of matter. Here Earth represents the solid state, Water the liquid or fluid state, Air the gaseous state and Fire the combustive, electric, ionised or plasmic state. The change from one state to another is illustrated by the fact if we apply Fire, i.e., heat, to Water, the water boils and the resultant steam is now a gaseous state of matter represented by the element Air. Similarly if we apply Fire to a metal represented by the element Earth it will probably melt the metal into the fluid state of matter represented by Water. Fire and Air are considered positive elements, faster and more active; they tend to rise upward and spread outward. Water and Earth are negative, slower and passive; they tend to fall, run together and collect at the lowest level (Water), or condense (Earth). One can construct a table running the gamut from activity to inertia as follows:

FIRE: Fastest, hottest, lightest. Ionisation. Combustion.   Activity

AIR: Fast, warm, light. Vaporisation. Evaporation.

WATER: Slow, cool, heavy. Liquefaction.

EARTH: Slowest, coldest, heaviest. Solidification.   Inertia

Such categories may be used to indicate many grades of experience. In his *A Guide for the Perplexed*, Ernst Schumacher uses such a structure to illustrate four 'Levels of Being', embracing the human, the animal, the vegetable and the mineral. Each level is separated from the one above or the one below by a growth or diminishment of a vital capacity.

The ubiquity and universality of such first principles are manifest at various levels. The primitive logic is inescapable. Even at the mundane level of, say, heating a house, electricity we can see would come under the rubric Fire, gas under Air, oil under Water and coal or wood under Earth. One is assigning 'particulars' to their relevant 'universals' and one can see at once that it presents little difficulty. Suppose we apply the elements to molecular states of matter. In solids (Earth) molecules are packed tight and strongly held together. In liquids (Water) molecules slide over each other but cling to each other in motion. In gases (Air) molecules lose their clinging qualities and move freely and rapidly in all directions. If enclosed they spread and occupy the whole enclosure. The average velocity of air molecules is over 1,000 miles an hour. In combustion (Fire) they split up into their constituent atoms where the limit of velocity is the speed of light. There is a progression from cohesion to detachment, from slowness to rapidity, from low to high temperature. Like space and time, structure and function form a continuum. One can regard structure as a slow, compacted form of function, function as a rapid, loosened up form of structure. Air, though generally formless, shows a potentiality for form in a whirlwind or tornado, Water in a whirlpool or vortex. Only in Earth, solid matter, does distinctive, enduring form manifest itself. The following table may be helpful:

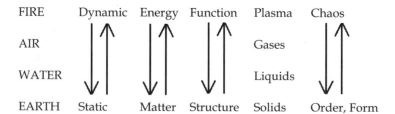

FIRE	Dynamic	Energy	Function	Plasma	Chaos
AIR				Gases	
WATER				Liquids	
EARTH	Static	Matter	Structure	Solids	Order, Form

To go back to Ernst Schumacher, his use of Plato's framework is intended to demonstrate the relationship between four levels of being. The lowest level, corresponding to the element Earth, is inanimate, inert, the next above it animate and capable of restricted movement if only instinctive, the level above that is that of conscious movement, while the human level (Fire) is characterised by self-awareness and a capacity for rational detachment, intuition or contemplation. The vital capacities – life, consciousness and self-awareness, are represented by x, y and z respectively so that the human level may be written as Mineral + x + y + z, the animal level by Mineral + x + y, the vegetable level by Mineral + x, and the mineral level simply by M. Schumacher remarks that x, y and z are invisible and impalpable. Only the solid mineral (Earth) level is the source of sense-data. Suppose we erect a table:

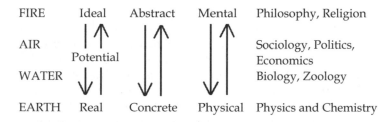

FIRE	Ideal	Abstract	Mental	Philosophy, Religion
AIR	Potential			Sociology, Politics, Economics
WATER				Biology, Zoology
EARTH	Real	Concrete	Physical	Physics and Chemistry

It should be noted that in strict terms science is confined to the bottom line. It has a foothold in the line above with biology, but sociology, politics and economics could scarcely be described as sciences. The bottom line is measurable and quantifiable. Above that we are in the realm of the qualifiable. The bottom line is concerned with 'hard fact', at least until the advent of quantum theory and relativity. It is the scene of reductionism and materialism. Above this line facts begin to get a little 'fuzzy'. Higher up we forsake the safer footholds of 'fact' for the less secure handholds of imagination, doubt and belief. At the same time the narrower, more precise begins to give way to the broader, more complex and indefinite. It is as though in this Platonic keyboard scale, ranging from the particular and finite to the general and infinite, human nature were a movable, percussive, finger.

Another version of this Platonic quadripartite elemental scheme is proposed by Robert Pirsig in his book, *Lila, An Enquiry into Morals*.

Roughly summarised, it is tabulated as follows:

Intellectual	Mind	Subjective	Mind	Intellectually alive	Undetermined
Social	Mind	Subjective	Mind	Socially alive	
Biological	Matter	Objective	Body	Physically alive	
Inorganic	Matter	Objective	Body	Inanimate. Dead.	Determined

There is a hierarchical order between free-will and determinism, mind and matter and, according to Pirsig, the tetralogy can be seen as levels of evolution. The top two levels and the bottom two are contained within each other – mind is contained in inorganic patterns, matter is contained in intellectual patterns. The four levels are static. The dynamism is supplied by what he calls a 'metaphysics of quality' in which mechanical causation is replaced by preference. Not only the top two lines can choose but also the bottom two. Even the inorganic, which one considers to be inanimate, may yet have some measure of choice, however restricted, as, for instance, whether to go through a slit marked particle or another marked wave. Obviously the extent of the possibility of choice is a factor of the evolutionary level. Pirsig claims that causation is a metaphysical term that can be replaced by 'value'. 'To say that "A causes B" or to say that "B values precondition A" is to say the same thing ... the only difference between causation and value is that the word "cause" implies absolute certainty whereas the implied meaning of "value" is one of preference.'

If causation is fundamentally a question of value, of quality, then ethics could be seen as a ground of 'Becoming', i.e., that the universe is at bottom a moral one. Willing as one may be to embrace the unconventional, an ethical universe would appear difficult to swallow. It would, however, not be an entirely new idea. If I understand Plato's *Timaeus* correctly, the ultimate aim was always 'the Good', the 'megiston mathema', the highest or greatest knowledge, which in Plato's view was undoubtedly ethical. The idea of a sub-atomic particle, freed from the push–pull of mechanical causation, being able to prefer or choose what it should do next, is a fascinating one, and that it should prefer the better of possible choices is even stranger. Can one have choice without animation? Or are, perhaps, not only viruses but even particles animate? The slender boundary between animate and inanimate seems, with the advance of science, almost at times to disappear. Is, then, the universe alive – an all-embracing ethical cosmos?

Perhaps this is a test as to how literally or imaginatively one takes it – as metaphor, a transference of meaning of possibly heuristic value, or as fact, if one can still believe in facts. Credo quia absurdum. Who knows? One is persuaded to consider that even apparently absurd ideas should be investigated rather than summarily dismissed. The history of history surely demands as much. Question everything, especially the insufficiently questioned established world of appearances which we are condemned to inhabit.

The Platonic scale we have illustrated above was also employed by the scientist–engineer A. M. Young in his book *The Reflexive Universe* to illustrate evolution not only in Darwinian, biological terms but also that of the individual body and mind. Young was a graduate of Princeton in mathematics. He was taught by one of the most eminent mathematicians of the day, Oswald Veblen, argued with Bertrand Russell and was influenced by the work of Ernst Cassirer. In his engineering capacity he was the inventor of the Bell helicopter.

Young made use of the elemental Platonic scale much as Schumacher and Pirsig did but in a more physical, biological way.

Young's method involved a descent down the scale and a rise up through it, as the accompanying diagram shows, though his version makes use of straight lines in a broad V rather than a sinus curve as shown here. If one remembers Plato's tetrad, Fire (light), Air, Water, Earth in descending order, Young takes light as the origin of

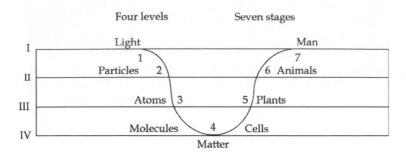

The left-hand descent is inanimate. The right-hand ascent is animate. To stage four we could perhaps assign viruses, half-way between the inanimate and animate. There is a microscopic increase on the left, a macroscopic increase on the right. The left-hand descent also can be seen as a deceleration of speed, the right-hand as an acceleration of movement, the left-hand as a progressive constriction of freedom, the right as an opening up of freedom.

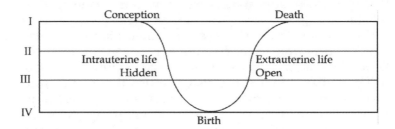

The intrauterine existence is an abridged version, recapitulation, of the past history of the species. The extrauterine life builds on, or extrapolates, the past history of the species. Both pre-natal and post-natal growth are subject to environmental influences. There is no such thing as a genetic type developing in the absence of an environment. Heredity supplies the possibilities while environment decides which of them will be actualised. The deceleration of the speed of growth of embryo and foetus mirrors the deceleration of speed from light to molecules and solid matter in the previous diagram.

everything descending from the abstract through ever increasing concretion through the gaseous form of matter, then the liquid form, and finally the solid form represented by the element Earth. It also demonstrates a descent in temperature from heat to cold, a progressive restriction of range of movement on the physical level, a similar progression from theory to fact on a mental level, and on both levels a gradation from freedom to necessity or determinism. Compare this descent and ascent with Goethe's idea of 'levity' as an opposing force to 'gravity'. On the downward path we have gravitation, on the upward, levitation.

At the bedrock of the element 'Earth' matter and matters become firmly established, 'down to earth', factual. This is the material level of hard matter and rigorous empiricism, of verifiable and reductionist science. But the curve does not stay there. Unable to go any lower, it begins to rise through the levels again. There are seven stages – three down – base – three up, so that Newton's colour spectrum and the musical scale could also be accommodated here. In Young's schema, however, the descent is inanimate and mechanical. It is also a fall from universal to particular, from idea to fact. Ideas are form-free; facts owe their factuality to form, particularly the cube which Plato ascribed to the element Earth. The 'Platonic or perfect solid' is an epitome of form.

The ascent starts with a change of form, a loosening of rigorous constriction, a gradual freeing up of what was concentrated, solid and inert. In contrast to the descent, the ascent is increasingly animate. Life begins and reaches upward toward the light. It 'levitates'. From physics and chemistry we move up to the life-embracing sciences, biology, zoology, anthropology, to the life of plants, animals and man. As we ascend, not only freedom of movement, but all freedoms, increase. The animal has more freedom than the plant; man has more freedom than either of the former. The seven stages are not the seven ages of man but the seven stages of evolution. The eighth stage, an octave, is not shown and indeed not known. Could it signify a new type of life, the curve to the right indicating what we imagine as future, that to the left what we remember as past? Young does not suggest this and stops at Man on level one, not humanity in all its frailty but in its fullest potential yet to be realised. However, elsewhere in the book a further existence after death is not put out of court.

We have to remember Plato's warning in *The Timaeus*. We are not dealing here with things but with concepts and with symbols for forming concepts. These can be considered as 'universals'. Existence may depend on them but existence is a state of the 'particular', not the 'universal'. Another caveat is suggested by the anthropologist Gregory Bateson which is not obvious in the diagrams – 'Living systems are not linear. Mathematics, logic, dead systems are linear.' Living systems are cyclic or helical.

Can we apply such co-ordinates meaningfully in any field we choose? Suppose, to go back to Cassirer's meridian–horizon cross, we look at the political scene briefly mentioned earlier. Here the vertical axis may stand for hierarchical structures, the horizontal for an egalitarian framework. The former is internal and individual with a tendency to autocratic behaviour, the latter external and social inclining to a democratic philosophy. Generally speaking, right-wing politicians tend to follow the vertical diameter. They believe in the importance of the status of birth, in inheritance, individual worth as opposed to social well-being, domination for themselves and subjection for others, property as a personal asset, not as a right for all. They tend to support class division, race division, sex division, income division, coupled with the intimacy of a superior breed seeing their peers as 'one of us'. Out of this mind-set, for aspirants are as much if not more so influenced as centuries-old landowners, grows class difference and its accompanying snobbery, apartheid, private hospitals and schools, the belief in imperialism, the maintenance of hereditary peerages and the flummery of tradition, bowing and curtseying and swearing allegiance to the crown. Left-wing politicians, on the other hand, proclaim democracy and equality, both qualities represented on the horizontal axis. They tend to be ostensibly more concerned for social welfare, for minimising inequalities in the distribution of wealth, for abolishing or radi-

cally changing the House of Lords. They tend to support
state schools and hospitals and public transport, at least in
theory, for those financially able frequently abandon principle in practice. The master–servant relationship beloved
of the vertical fraternity does not enthral them. All should
be treated equally, at least in theory, though this rarely
happens even when the Left manages to get power and
form a government. While the Right when in power sticks
to what it calls its principles, even if they are no more than
prejudices, the Left, on the other hand, seems only too
eager to give them up, appearing to think that when it is
in power it too is a sort of aristocracy and must act as
such, with the result that any government, even one of the
Left, tends to conservatism. As Bertrand Russell has
remarked, in Sicily during the war with Carthage, the rich
favoured oligarchy, the poor democracy, but when the
supporters of democracy got the upper hand their leader
usually became a tyrant. This is a danger for all left-wing
governments seduced by the panoply of power.

We can take the logic a little further. On the vertical axis
we can say that superiority has its place on the upper pole,
inferiority on the lower, while equal worth has its place on
the horizontal axis. We have already noted that the vertical may relate to inner or mental, the horizontal to the
outer or physical. It would appear then that superiority
and inferiority are basically internal, individual or mental
ideas whereas egalitarianism, parity and fair shares are an
external, environmental or social aspect of the structure.
The inference is that hierarchy is not for society; it is for
the individual. It embraces ideas of better or worse,
higher or lower, an internal ethical ladder *within the individual*. Egalitarianism is external, for society, for relationships with others. It carries with it ideas of equality, justice, sharing, participating and so on. It is a social quality
between people. The trouble comes when each set of qualities operates in its wrong field, the individual in the social
and vice versa. Egalitarianism in the individual, internal
field leads to mediocrity, vacillation and loss of decision –
one thing is as good as another. Hierarchy in the external,
social field invites domination and submission, oppres-
sion, excess opulence and penury, class distinction and

class war. Hierarchy is an individual virtue but a social vice. Egalitarianism is an individual vice but a social virtue. It must surely be regretfully recognised that down the centuries and across the world for much of the time and in most places each quality series has been operating in its wrong field.

We have dealt with Cassirer's meridian–horizon cross and with Plato's four elemental levels. These four levels, however, contained seven stages. Structure and function appear to resonate to the number seven almost as much as to four. Examples are the seven days of the week, the seven planets associated with them, the metals associated with the planets, the colour spectrum and the musical scale.

Seven, as we have remarked elsewhere, is an extraordinary number. Just how odd it is can be gleaned by a study of The Book of Revelation. The 'seven stars', the 'seven churches' in Asia, the 'seven golden candlesticks' are only three examples of the ubiquity of this strange number. Seven is the only number from one to ten which does not divide into the 360 degree circle without a fraction, and even the fraction is a recurring decimal repeating itself into infinity. The number 360 divided by seven gives us 51.42857142857142857 for ever. If we divide not 360 degrees but the 365 days of the year by seven it gives us 52.142857, there being just over 52 weeks in the year, and we see the mysterious 142857 cropping up again.

Suppose we set out a seven-fold table for the seven metals which alchemy allotted to the sun, moon and five planets, lead to Saturn, tin to Jupiter, iron to Mars, gold to sun, mercury to Mercury, copper to Venus and silver to moon. If we now rate these metals according to resonance (timbre when struck), lustre (brightness in light reflection) and conductivity for heat and for electricity we have:

Silver
Copper
Mercury
Gold
Iron
Tin
Lead

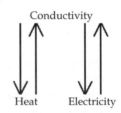

Resonance   Lustre   Heat   Electricity

Here lead is the least resonant, least bright and worst conductor while silver is the most resonant (bell-like), most reflective and the best conductor. The positions of the other metals indicate their relative susceptibility. Mercury as fluid is an exception but when frozen occupies its correct position in the scale. The bottom two can be cast but not forged, the top two forged but not cast, the middle three can be both cast and forged.

This table also corresponds with the angular velocity of the corresponding planets with their revolution round the sun. The top three are the swiftest, the bottom three the slowest, by far the swiftest being the moon (silver) and the slowest Saturn (lead). In the seven colours of the rainbow – the colour spectrum – the sky is red at sunset because sunlight has to travel through more of the atmosphere to reach us – red is related to density and relatively low frequency (long wavelength). The blue end of the spectrum ending in violet renders the sky blue since the relatively high frequency and short wavelength scatters sunlight in all directions, striking on molecules, particles and water and ice from clouds. Here in order from the highest frequency to the lowest we have the seven colours of the spectrum – Violet, Indigo, Blue, Green, Yellow, Orange and Red. In music, too, the seven notes of the Tonic Sol-Fa relate to rising and falling scales of wave-frequency.

Structures give form to function just as function brings life to structure. The idea that life evolved according to what may be described as pattern is an old one. It was implicit in Plato's 'Forms' where what was actual and particular copied or participated in what was ideal or universal. It was taken up and expanded by that forerunner of the theory of evolution, Aristotle. It was revived by the Greek physician Galen in his 'dynamis diaplastike' or formative force. It surfaced again in rather different form in Paracelsus's *Archaeus*, and a little later by Kepler in his 'facultas formatrix' or formative faculty. Goethe re-echoed the idea in his 'Urpflanze' or archetypal plant-form. More recently we have had Driesch's 'entelechy', von Bertalanffy's systems theory, Lancelot Law Whyte's 'morphic principle', the ideas of the anthro-

pologist Gregory Bateson and the biologist Rupert
Sheldrake's 'morphic resonance'.

Beyond Appearances

In Indian philosophy the world was seen as Maya – illusion. In Western philosophy Kant described it as phenomena – appearances. To Prospero 'we are such stuff as dreams are made on'. What lies behind the illusion, the appearance, the dreams? Is there anything at all behind them? Appearance is reality because we have nothing but appearance to go on. It is all we have – the thing as it appears to us. The 'thing in itself' behind the appearance is, as Kant maintained, unknowable, if indeed it exists. Are we merely shadow-boxing? Are the interstellar galaxies and nebulae that our telescopes and calculations discover for us actual entities or mere appearances? One cannot deny their appearance unless one is blind, but is there anything beyond the appearance?

It has been remarked that our sense organs, besides enabling us to realise our world, appreciate and live in it, disable us from appreciating more. Without our senses our world would not exist for us, but it is also limited to what our senses tell us. Our senses are more than organs of experience; they are also organs of limitation. They shut us out from that which they themselves are not constructed to interpret. All we can perceive is what our minds and sensory-motor equipment allow us to perceive. The universe as we see it from sub-atomic particle to Andromeda and the Pole Star depends on the inadequate equipment nature has provided us with. Telescopes and microscopes are, after all, but extensions of eyes and without eyes would be useless. We would live in a world of touch, taste, smell and noise but without light, colour or perspective, and no inkling of Andromeda or the electron. Our sense organs permit us to experience only that part of reality that is of use to us, allows us a little room for imagination and experiment and ensures our continued existence.

The universe as we know it depends on us, as we in turn depend on it, for we live in this fabrication of ours. It supports us as we support it – appearance depending on appearance. We are tailored to each other – we and our world. If this is so there must be other worlds, for experience is not limited to human beings. A dog's world we must assume is a much smaller world than ours but it is still a palpable, visible world to a dog, a world in which the sense of smell is sharpened, its sight and colour sense dulled, its perspective undeveloped, bringing forth a very different world from ours though still containing the trees and lamp-posts common to us both. The world of a dinosaur we must imagine was even more restricted. There are obviously many different worlds, each conjured up out of the available sense equipment. We can only wonder at the world of the sea anemone; we can never experience it.

Our view of our world is tied to the mind and sense organs of the descendants of apes, a tiny, infinitesimal group in the history and cosmography of the universe. It is surely taking egocentricity to extremes to assume that this insignificant creature, man, a pin-point in the immensity of space and time, has the key to the riddle of the universe, that what he perceives, or will eventually be able to perceive with his limited equipment, is literally all there is. Yet this is not just the attitude of the common man; it is also that of probably the majority of scientists. The 'Big Bang' merchants and the Stephen Hawkings of this world already seem to think they are well on the way to the answer and that it is only a matter of time. That such millennial optimism has flourished again and again in history, only to be repeatedly discounted, does not appear to trouble them. They work on what can be seen, measured, reasoned and counted and within that narrow compass believe they will have the answer to all. We have seen it all before and are yet apparently little wiser.

If we have no proof of other worlds it may well be because, like the sea anemone, we are not equipped to discover them, not because they do not exist. Indeed some people, often dismissed as simple-minded or superstitious in the cold light of reason, appear to have what might be described as a sixth sense by means of which they claim to have access to at least one other world, an extra sense now popularised by the initials ESP – extra-sensory perception. Such a claim is highly unwelcome to, if not denied by, most scientists since within the conventions that dominate scientific thought it is an impossibility, and indeed no one seems to have located the seat of this 'sixth sense'. It cannot be discovered by the other senses which form the basis of science, so scientifically it does not exist. It can be conceived by the mind but the mind, unlike the brain, is insubstantial and again cannot be measured, seen or touched. The fact that the mind is as much a basis for science as our senses is ignored since it is too uncomfortable to be entertained. For it means that the foundations of science are themselves insubstantial, cannot be weighed, measured or counted and are therefore unscientific. Science which counters belief with fact is itself founded on belief. In Goethe's words, 'Alles faktisches schon Theorie ist' – All fact is already theory.

Let us bring our world down to a more manageable size. If we look at another person we see his body moving, his face smiling or frowning, his eyes blinking, but the person himself is invisible. We can see his body much better than he can himself. That is appearance; that is real. But that is not all there is. We know from our own experience and from analogy that there is something beyond the appearance; there is the person himself though we can never know his invisible self except by making guesses at it from signs and motions he expresses to the outside world. Moreover some of these may be feigned and intended to deceive. All his thoughts, feelings, ideas and fantasies are hidden from us yet, since we have them ourselves, we must assume they are there. We do not only not know him; we can never really know him. We have constructed his exterior appearance out of our sense organs but we have not constructed him. Nor indeed has he constructed himself out of his own sense organs, his body perhaps, but not his mind, his emotions, hopes and wishes, fears and despairs. There is more to man than sense. Does not this suggest that there is more beyond appearance than appearance suggests? And if so can we apply the same thinking to our apparent world? Is there not perhaps an inner invisible world that we cannot experience because we have not the equipment (whatever that might mean in human terms) to comprehend it? Could there not be perhaps several other worlds – worlds within worlds – interpenetrating, interlacing with ours and yet distinct? This might go some way to explain perhaps the inexplicable occurrences of extra-sensory perception, of immaterial apparitions such as ghosts which normally sane people have claimed they saw, or the strange happenings recorded in C. G. Jung's autobiography, all of which have been dismissed as fantasy because to our rational minds our apparent world is incapable of accommodating them. The pragmatist philosopher and psychologist William James thought that 'our normal waking consciousness, rational consciousness, is but one special type of consciousness, while all about it, parted from it by the flimsiest of screens, there are potential forms of consciousness entirely different'.

In his Doctrine of Forms Plato talked of 'saving the appearances' (sōzein ta phenomena). To him phenomena were particulars beyond which lay universals, the universals being more real than the particulars, i.e., the Ideas or Forms were more real than the phenomena (appearances). The Ideas were objective, universally recognisable while the phenomena were subjective appearances and relative to the individual observer whether human being or sea anemone. The phenomena were implicated in the Ideas in two ways, by participation (methexis) and by imitation (mimēsis). The appearances were in essence a material exposition of aspects of the ideal Forms. On the shoulders of Plato, what I am suggesting here is that our phenomenal world is not the only world participating in the Ideas and that there may be others. If we have no proof it may well be because we are not equipped to discover them, not because they do not exist. Our equipment is limited.

I would like to go further and venture the idea that the appearance we take to be real is in fact allegorical, an allegory of something else, and that meaning is concealed in the appearance. I suggest that the appearances, the phenomena, are 'theatrical scenery', both hiding and hinting at a deeper significance. Behind the mask is the player. Behind the player is the character to be played. Behind the character is the plot and behind that the author. We watch what the play presents to us and assume it has meaning. We assume it because we know the author, or know of him, and we make sense or nonsense of it in that light. We are assured, however, by those who should know, the scientists (since science means knowledge), that our world is no theatre, has no play, no author and no meaning. All there is is appearance which they dignify with the word 'fact', forgetting that facts are unavoidably subjective and to that extent unscientific.

It is not suggested that we can all read 'books in the running brooks' or 'sermons in stones' but we might perhaps consider our phenomenal world as a sort of parable, a stage not of mere scenery, masks and props, but a theatre of meaning. Furthermore I would like to suggest that there might be more than one such theatre. The universe is a much larger, stranger and more subtle construction than our Hubble telescopes and electron microscopes can ever present us with, and we have not even mentioned the problem of time. If we go further we will be set on a voyage of improbability. Nothing is proven; nothing will be proved. We can only experience. It is seeking, not finding, that is the more important, and possibly understanding. There would seem to be one essential admonition – to keep an open mind.

Three Patterns of Love

Structure and function are applicable to emotional life. Let us take love. There are three main kinds of love typified by the Greek words – Eros, Philia and Agapē. Eros is personal, physical and sensual, basically structured by differences in structure of the male and female body. It can be reduced, however, to self-love or expanded to physical love of another of the same sex. All the senses are excited but the predominant sense is that of touch, especially of primary and secondary sex organs, and of lips, also of skin surfaces. It has an immediate aim of giving pleasure either to another or to oneself through orgasm or ecstasy. Its remoter aim is philoprogenitive, the generation of children. It is the most basic of the forms of love, physically uniting opposite sexes, without which the world would have no future.

The second form of love, Philia (or Philadelphia, 'brotherly love'), varies from affection to friendship. It may be enhanced by physical contact – the kiss of greeting – but does not depend on it. It can be carried on at a distance whereas erotic love needs sexual contact. If one could describe erotic love as electromagnetic then the love of Philia is gravitational. One is inclined rather than forcibly attracted. As the weaker force gravity can operate from a distance just as the force of gravity in nature operates, whereas the stronger force, the electromagnetic, as again in nature, is immediate in both a temporal and spatial sense. In Philia, if the immediate magnetism is missing, the inclination is nevertheless capable of strength and endurance. The love of Philia relates to the structure of one's relationship with others, with family, friends and society. It tends to manifest itself in friendship, altruism, solidarity, comradeship, fellow feeling, parental and filial love. It is the cement of society. Marriage is a combination of Eros and Philia. When the physical magnetic attrac-

24

tion fades the enduring inclination of Philia may yet hold it together.

Agapē is the third kind of love. It is the word for love used by St. Paul in his paean on love in Corinthians I.13. It is sometimes translated as 'charity', as it is indeed in St. James's Bible. Agapē is much broader and all-embracing than either Eros or Philia. It is also weaker and far less common. Few people, it seems, can manage it. Eros is largely between couples. Philia is more expansive and includes friends, colleagues and communities. Agapē embraces everyone without distinction and also includes compassion, which is why, no doubt, the translators of the Bible chose to construe it as 'charity'. But if one consults Liddell and Scott's *Greek Lexicon* one reads that charity is the second meaning. The first meaning is love. If the love of Eros is electromagnetic while that of Philia is gravitational, then that of Agapē is, in Goethe's sense, 'levitational', outward and upward.

The absence of Eros may develop into personal hate. The absence of Philia may degenerate into dislike, disapproval, detestation or indifference. The absence of Agapē is the common lot of mankind in general. Few are apparently aware of its existence, let alone of its absence. Love and hate play an important part in the blending of the four elements – Fire, Air, Water and Earth – according to Empedocles. They blended with each other in the fabrication of the cosmos as in Plato's *Timaeus*. But what brought about the blending, or indeed their disassociation? The answer, for Empedocles, was the forces of Love and Hate which can be interpreted as Harmony and Discord or, in modern physical terms, as the electromagnetic forces of Attraction and Repulsion.

We can see such forces working themselves out not only in the physics of electromagnetism, in chemical change and biological metabolism, but also in social, political, economic and international life. We cannot escape them. They are part of us as they are of our world. Only one of the three forms of love escapes its negative opposite – hate or dislike. It is Agapē. While in intention universal, Agapē is the weakest force of the three. Indeed it is hardly a 'force' at all. It does not belong to the world of action and reaction. It 'turns the other cheek'. It bypasses the materialism of Earth, instinct (Water), reason (Air) and reaches out toward understanding beyond intuition (Fire). It is the Quinta Essentia, the fifth principle, the quintessence which brings the other four together. Not surprisingly, with its all-embracing frailty, it is as rare as its position at the top of the scale suggests. For most of the world it would not appear to exist at all, and certainly not for its rulers, whether political or economic, who manage, at our expense, quite nicely without it.

Iris Murdoch, who died recently, wrote in her *Metaphysics as a Guide to Morals* that Schopenhauer was probably aware of the difference between kinds of love – 'Perhaps Schopenhauer followed a Buddhist path in making compassion the prime virtue.' Compassion is not a thing of the moment or of enduring proximity but of unremitting, universal application. Unlike Eros or Philia, which both have a certain limiting structure, Agapē has none. It is almost pure function – formless, timeless, class-less, sexless, boundless. It embraces the sinner as much as the saint, the beggar as much as the beggarer. It makes no distinction between black and white, between race or nation, between rich or poor, friend or enemy. While Eros connotes an intoxicating adherent uniting body with body, Philia a milder cohesive compound conjoining family and friends, Agapē is spread thinly throughout humanity in general, often so scantily that it is barely dis-cernible. It is, nevertheless, the sine qua non of universal peace and good will. It is the source and anchor of any universal ethic. It was exemplified by the Buddha and has been extolled by prophets and mystics down the ages, usually to little effect. It is, in essence, the goal of all mystics – the unification of The All with The One. It is the negation of structure since structure is confining and lim-iting. Compassion is the feeling, the emotion and action of which mysticism is the inner, intuitive equivalent.

Agapē, compassion, is a 'Yea-Sayer'. It denies no one. Mysticism, on the other hand, is negative. It follows the 'Neti-Neti', the 'not this' of Hinduism. It seeks the Love of Jacob Boehme that 'may fitly be compared to Nothing for it is deeper than any thing'. It is manifest in this couplet of

Angelus Silesius:

'Gott ist ein lauter Nichts, ihn rührt kein Nun noch Hier;
je mehr du nach ihm greiffst, je mehr entwind er dir'.
(God is a pure Nothing, not moved by Now and Here;
the more thou seekst to grasp Him, the more He escapes
thee.)

But, as in Chuang-Tzu, Heraclitus and Hegel, the positive and negative are versions of the same. They come together in Heraclitus's 'harmony in contrariety', or in the synthesis of Hegel's dialectic achieved by his 'Methode der Absoluten Negativität'. The two opposite poles meet in the centre – in The One. 'That art Thou', the Upanishads teach us, and that, essentially, is the meaning of Agapē.

We have noted elsewhere the reciprocal nature of structure and function. As the one waxes, the other wanes, as in wavelength and frequency. So it is with love. Where Eros is all pervading, Agapē barely exists. Eros is particular; Agapē aims at but never reaches the universal. Eros is 'earthy', necessary, occupying the lowest rung of Plato's ladder. Agapē is of the spirit, of free-will, approaching the top rung. In Cassirer's meridian–horizon cross, since it is a question of ethics it is the vertical axis which is pertinent. Eros occupies the factual, deterministic (driven by libido and the forces of evolution) and particular lower pole. Agapē encamps on the optional, insubstantial, absolute and universal upper pole.

The reciprocity of structure and function is perhaps the basis of the tendency of many mystics to avoid Eros and embrace the solitary or celibate life. Some philosophers such as Plato, Kant, Schopenhauer and Nietzsche do much the same. William Blake and Bertrand Russell however were not of that kidney, a mystic and a philosopher for whom Eros and Goethe's 'Ewig-Weibliche' appeared to have attractions.

The Music of the Spheres

One of the earliest advocates of order in the cosmos (cosmos in Greek means order) was Pythagoras. His idea of mathematical order, he claimed, reached its zenith in the 'music of the spheres', a cosmic harmony. This idea has been written off as romantic nonsense for so long now as to discourage further investigation in this field. However, a few fairly recent discoveries seem to add weight to the claim. There is, for instance, according to Professor Gerhard Krüger, a curious relationship between the planetary revolutions of the three outermost planets – Uranus, Neptune and Pluto – and that paragon of geometry, Pythagoras's theorem. It is not accurate, as in Euclid, since we are dealing with our phenomenal not an ideal world, but nevertheless close enough to make an inescapable point. The revolutionary period of Uranus is 84 years, of Neptune 165 years and of Pluto 249 years. 84 + 165 = 249. If we divide by ten we get 8.4 + 16.5 = 24.9. This is very close to 9 + 16 = 25 or $3^2 + 4^2 = 5^2$ which of course is the ratio of Pythagoras's theorem.

One can pursue this peculiar relationship diagrammatically.

Suppose we illustrate each revolution by a cube and arrange the cubes in pyramid form, both in elevation and in plan as illustrated.

The Uranus and Neptune pyramids have a flat base as if resting on the earth when seen in elevation. The Pluto pyramid, however, is a double pyramid in elevation, the 81 cubes of the ground level corresponding to the Neptunian 81 cubes at ground level while the Plutonian submerged 84 cubes correspond to the total of Uranian cubes, i.e., 84. It is left to the reader to get what he can out of this strange confirmation of Pythagorean planetary relationships.

The geophysicist Professor Rudolf Tomaschek pursues

The outer planets – Uranus, Neptune and Pluto.
Relationships of revolutionary periods in years as cubic steps in
pyramidical form. (After Professor Gerhard Krüger.)

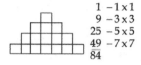

$$\begin{aligned}1 &- 1\times1\\9 &- 3\times3\\25 &- 5\times5\\\underline{49} &- 7\times7\\84&\end{aligned}$$

Uranus Pyramid. Elevation.

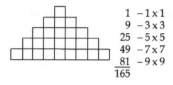

$$\begin{aligned}1 &- 1\times1\\9 &- 3\times3\\25 &- 5\times5\\49 &- 7\times7\\\underline{81} &- 9\times9\\165&\end{aligned}$$

Neptune Pyramid. Elevation.

Uranus Pyramid. Plan.

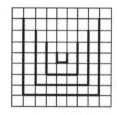

Neptune Pyramid. Plan.

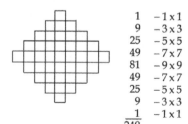

$$\begin{aligned}1 &- 1\times1\\9 &- 3\times3\\25 &- 5\times5\\49 &- 7\times7\\81 &- 9\times9\\49 &- 7\times7\\25 &- 5\times5\\9 &- 3\times3\\\underline{1} &- 1\times1\\249&\end{aligned}$$

Pluto Pyramid.
Elevation
(Double Pyramid).

The Pluto Pyramid is a double
pyramid. Its plan is the same as
the Neptune plan but its elevation
involves a Neptune Pyramid above
the surface and an inverted Uranus
Pyramid below it. Note that the
totals, 84, 165 and 249,
correspond with their respective
planetary revolutions in years.

the matter of planetary revolutions still further, pointing out that five revolutions of Jupiter (59.3 years) are comparable with two Saturn revolutions (58.9 years), two Uranus revolutions (168 years) approximate to one Neptune revolution (164.8 years) and three Uranus revolutions (252.1 years) correspond to one Pluto revolution (247.7 years). Again, as if that were not enough, three Neptune revolutions (494.4 years) relate to two Pluto revolutions (495.5 years). There is also a very curious relationship between certain planets and the mathematical ratio, 'pi' (π = 3.14159), involving the sidereal revolutions of the moon, Mercury, Mars, Jupiter and Saturn. The sidereal revolution is that measured against the fixed stars. Finally Professor N. Heitler FRS in *Man and Science* (Oliver & Boyd, 1963) has claimed that from the relationships between six planets of the solar system the whole major and minor scale can be discovered. In Frankfurt in 1974 Thomas Michael Schmidt published *Musik und Kosmos als Schöpfungswunder*, an extraordinary book in which music, mathematics and cosmic factors are shown to be interrelated and interwoven. It's a long story. Four hundred years ago Johannes Kepler found that the angular velocities of planets at perihelion and aphelion corresponded to a musical interval. Perhaps, after all, Pythagoras was right.

Patterns of History

There was an idea not uncommon in the eighteenth century and into the nineteenth that history, in addition to being a random concatenation of events, appeared to conform broadly with rational or physical laws. The apparent originator of this idea was the Neapolitan philosopher Giambattista Vico in his *Principi della Scienza Nuova*. He was followed by Hegel in his philosophy of history, by Marx in his dialectical materialism, by Spengler in *The Decline of the West* and by Arnold Toynbee in his twelve-volume *A Study of History*. There were others, perhaps not so closely identifiable but with a similar cast of thought. Lewis Mumford and Pitirim Alexandrovitch Sorokin come to mind. Isaiah Berlin, to whom the concept seemed to appear of interest if not congenial, added Montesquieu, Condorcet, Saint-Simon and Auguste Comte to their number. Even our own Buckle in his *History of Civilisation in England* devoted the first two chapters of his first volume to resources for investigating history and the influence of physical laws. In chapter four he deals with intellectual laws.

The Russian-American Sorokin evolved a schema based on the cycles of three systems. The first embraced an inward, quasi-mystical, ethical, almost religious principle, the second a materialist, outward, positivist view and both were combined in a third, synthetic, harmonising conception. Applied to the rise and decline of cultures or civilisations, the cyclic predominance of one or other of the above modes, it was claimed, coincided with the end or the radical inception of a new culture or civilisation. Sorokin's American contemporary, the writer and philosopher Lewis Mumford, ruthlessly criticised the 'arrogant dogmatism' of Spengler, the 'anti-historical other-worldliness' of Toynbee and considered Sorokin to 'combine the weakest features of both'. Yet Mumford himself was a believer in

31

the periodicity of cultures, as his numerous books eloquently testify.

That our philosophers of history arrived at different conclusions does not invalidate the idea of a basic periodic structure. It merely demonstrates that, for example, Vico was not Hegel and Vico's circumstances not those of the author of *The Philosophy of History*. To Hegel, 'the only thought which philosophy brings with it to the contemplation of history is the simple conception of Reason; that Reason is the sovereign of the world; that the history of the world, therefore, presents us with a rational process'. Hegel's philosophy of history, as Bertrand Russell has remarked, is 'partly the effect, and partly the cause, of the teaching of world history in German schools'. Vico, Hegel, Marx, Toynbee and the rest cannot be considered without relation to circumstance. Each reads the text through his own spectacles, in his own study and in his own time and climate of belief. Moreover, history does not follow 'laws' of development, though perhaps it may respond to clues or signposts.

Nevertheless, what seems to bring them together is the idea of an underlying rational framework which, if it does not determine the course of history, and obviously it does not, may all the same serve as a speculative navigating instrument by means of which those voyaging through the seas of space and time can come to some appreciation of approximately where they are and can set their course on a compass bearing which may bring them within a few hundred miles of the Never-Never Land they have their eyes on. The navigating instrument is, of course, both a conscious concept and a subconscious intuition. Nothing happens as deterministic accuracy would have it. Individual events happen because they have room for manoeuvre in the ever-changing interstices of the structure. Yet, broadly speaking the framework may make itself felt, however vaguely and approximately.

That proponent of revolutionary syndicalism, Georges Sorel, an assiduous reader and critic of Vico, believed that laws of nature, such as they were, could be used as strategic instruments perhaps, but not slavishly obeyed. He took the view that nature was chaotic, a savage jungle.

To him Vico took too much for granted. Taken literally, the idea that events may relate to mathematical cycles and structures can too easily be dismissed as nonsense. Napoleon's defeat at Waterloo was not a confirmation of a recurring cycle. It was not the result of celestial or terrestrial mathematics. It was not written in the stars. But that is not to say that there are no applicable cycles or rhythms at all, no critical periods, no diurnal, monthly, annual, centennial or other rhythms to which events appear to dance. The music, to which we give the name Zeitgeist, is there but an event is not obliged to dance to it though it may nevertheless feel the urge. And if, indeed, it does dance, it has its own idiosyncratic rhythm which may be a little out of step with the music of the time. Nothing in life is exact. There is no precise engaging of gears in a well-oiled machine. The relationship between the abstractions of mathematics, the potentialities of time and the concreteness of material events is a loose one. Hegel put it down to reason. But there is little looseness about logic.

(The background to the above I owe largely to Isaiah Berlin's essay on Vico in *Against the Current.*)

Prospero's Metaphor

Alles Vergängliche	All that is transitory
Ist nur ein Gleichnis	Is but a metaphor.
Das Unzulängliche	The Inaccessible
Hier wird's Ereignis.	Becomes here actuality.

– Goethe, *Faust*

We have mentioned elsewhere the belief that the phenomenal world, the world of transient things, which to us seems the real world, is really a metaphor, an allegory. The metaphorical view, which has been increasingly corroborated by the advance of science, which reluctantly has been forced, by its own brilliant progress, to question the materiality of matter, is now becoming a real problem for scientists. The palpability is really no more than sense-data, and their much-prized objectivity has proved to be ill founded. Facts have dissolved under scrutiny and science is in danger of becoming a faculty of art. Those first explorers of the mysteries of life, the poets, have long found 'tongues in trees, books in the running brooks, sermons in stone'. From the beginning they have realised that nature is, in Prospero's words in *The Tempest*, 'an insubstantial pageant'.

If, as Goethe claimed, our world is a metaphor, while Shakespeare called it an 'insubstantial pageant', suppose we take them at their word. Our world then becomes a living drama – 'all the world's a stage'. What we perceive, our world of mountains, seas, rivers and cities, is in effect stage scenery. We ourselves are actors in a play. We are off stage when asleep or on another stage when we are dreaming. We act a part which has been written for us at conception and birth but then have the freedom to interpret our part in our own way, a limited free-will, circumscribed by the everpresence of the environment and by the free-will and determinism of others. The author of the play is to us unknown. Some say there is no author. To them it has all been knit together, timed, programmed and framed by Chance with no conceivable purpose in it – a materialist miracle. But if materialism has been shown to be the underwear of the Emperor's New Clothes, then where does that leave us?

Our play has a broad script or text but nevertheless has room for development, shall we say 'evolution'. The laws of such evolution are, as we have suggested of the laws of physics, more signposts than rigid precepts or prohibitions. They allow for the variation of involvement and development so that we as players are not just mechanical puppets but can play our part in the development. The drama evolves guided by broad, general structures and the timing of nature. It has no detectable origin and no final curtain. It grows, and the way it grows depends to some extent on what we, the players, put into it. The text we have been handed at birth is susceptible to extension and new addition to some degree through our personal participation. We are not only actors programmed to interpret a given script but also part authors environmentally influenced to evolve it.

If this is so, one might well ask, to what end? For there is a distinct teleological aspect to any such suggestion. What's it all for? The answer would seem to be, as to other questions in this book – a question mark. No one knows. The evolutionary philosopher Henri Bergson (author of *L'Évolution Créatrice*) held the belief that the universe was an instrument for the perfection of humanity. If so, we are participants in attempting to achieve that end. But who wrote the 'software'? Is the author outside our drama or within it? Does the play write itself? Should we be monotheist, polytheist, pantheist or atheist? Depending on what we mean by such terms, the question, one suspects, is not susceptible to answer and probably never will be. The easiest way out of the difficulty is to ascribe it all to chance, to accident, and have done with it. But that is even more unbelievable than purpose, where you are never 'done with it', for it opens up endless vistas. Should we not, then, settle for an open mind? Certainty, like perfection, is not achievable this side of the grave and, possibly, if there is another side, not even then.

It Can't All Be Make-believe, Can It?

The structures we have been describing are also fictions as man-made as the appearances to which we relate them. We are indeed 'shadow-boxing' in a world of make-believe, a world to which we are condemned by the anthropomorphic sensory-motor equipment and minds with which we are of necessity equipped. It is a world in which the appearance of reality depends on us as we, in turn, are dependent on it. We prop each other up.

Can we reach beyond appearance to something we could perhaps call reality? Is there anything at all beyond appearance? Here I can do no more than state my personal feeling. There is, of course, no proof. It is beyond reason. Reason relates to phenomena and stops there, whether the appearances are sensual or mental. In *The Timaeus* Plato described his cosmological vision not as fact but as 'a likely story', a parable or metaphor. I have described myself as an 'agnostic' – one who doesn't know. But one can have 'hunches', feelings, 'intimations of immortality', as Wordsworth put it, that go beyond reason. Though one cannot *prove* anything, no one can disprove it either. Among my hunches is the idea that everything has meaning. It may be concealed in the appearance but nevertheless decipherable if one recognises it and is prepared to do a little detective work. Following on from this, if life has a meaning it would seem counterproductive to conclude that it was nevertheless purposeless. What is the point of meaning without an aim for which meaning acts as a blueprint for achieving that aim?

It is equally conceivable, of course, that our world, our life has no meaning at all, no purpose, no stick behind it, no carrot before it, no first cause and no final cause; only, in Aristotle's terms, a *material* and *efficient* cause, and these due solely to chance, to accident. Things bump into each

other accidentally and lo and behold reassemble themselves into a human being, a symphony, a Taj Mahal or
Parthenon, a space-rocket or the Internet. I find this very
difficult to believe. Yet scientists for reasons of their own
still seem to believe it in spite of the new worlds opened
up to them by quantum physics. In the realm of neo-
Darwinism Professor Richard Dawkins still seems to
believe it, and there are many others. To my mind chance
and necessity are, like function and structure, indissolubly
linked. They are the materialistic equivalents of free-will
and determinism. Chance is an excess of function in a
determinist structure, necessity an excess of structure con-
trolling a free flow. Chance is a temporal variation, usually local, of a general determinism. Both are relative, not
absolute. In our world of appearances nothing is absolute.
In our body of appearances physiology and anatomy work
together, modifying each other, combining in a life-
enabling synthesis. So it is, I suggest, with chance and
necessity.

I'm inclined to believe therefore that appearance is not
all; that it is only a metaphor for some underlying or over-
arching principle of an ethical nature, that Socrates's
'Daimon' and Plato's 'The Good' were not idle phantasms
but signatures of a 'divine ground', a realm of Being to
which our Becoming is but a prelude. I take it that the role
of phenomena is to perform the part of an instructor to
that effect. The patterns we have discussed are means for
instilling some order into the metaphor to help with its
interpretation.

If anyone asks whether there is a God one must be precise about what one means by the word, and to be precise
is to be false since God cannot be described. It is beyond
reason, beyond words. As the Taoists say, 'the Tao that
can be named is not the true Tao'.

I have a hunch that there is a sort of all-pervading divine
principle, call it what you wish as long as you remember
that any such name restricts rather than explains, a principle from which everything flows and grows. It is outside time and space. It is eternal and everywhere at once
while at the same time it is Nothing, The Void. Opposites
no longer exist. There is just the One or the All, different

facets of the Same. Opposites arise out of appearances. It is not in the future for there is no future. It is here and now, behind the stage scenery which constitutes our world. It can be approached through the blinding flash of insight or illumination or worked towards in time through the metaphor of appearances, but when one has reached it time disappears.

This 'divine ground' or principle reaches, I suggest, into our lives by means of increasingly human 'tentacles', both mental and physical, enabling the ideal and the potential to reveal themselves in the actual (Aristotle's 'potentia' and 'actus'). The revelation is progressive, manifesting itself through personal phenomena in the form of a teacher such as a Buddha, a Christ or a Mahomet. This enables the seeker to transcend appearances and reach toward the real, the absolute, through the medium or channel of a chosen teacher. Each teacher has his own vision of, and communication with, the absolute, and this is externalised and codified in a religion. Since religions take on the traditions and the mind-set of the societies in which they arise and the historical period in which they are rooted, they tend to differ, however much their teachers may point to The One and The Same. Clothing religion in the garb and fashion of the time, place and society, while making it acceptable to that society, also obscures its reason for existence in pursuit of The One. The distorted structure perverts its function. Appearances appear much more real than reality. We are caught in the web of appearances that we ourselves have spun. We ourselves prevent ourselves from seeing behind the façade which we unwittingly have built. The façade, however, is not solely our construction. We may be the builders but the chief architect is the divine principle. Mixing our metaphors, the façade, the web of appearances, may be taken as an instance of a collaboration between phenomenon and noumenon, between appearance and essence, The Many and The One. Or so it seems to me. But the reader should not take my word for it. He or she will no doubt have his or her own interpretation.

There seems no way in which this essence behind appearance can be described, though people have tried.

Mystics, for instance, have tried to put into words that which is essentially indescribable. On the realisation of Nirvana the Buddha is reported to have said (*The Tibetan Book of the Dead*), 'There is, disciples, a Realm devoid of earth and water, fire and air. It is not endless space, nor infinite thought, nor nothingness, neither ideas nor non-ideas. Not this world nor that is it. I call it neither a coming nor a departing, nor a standing still, nor death, nor birth; it is without a basis, progress or a stay; it is the ending of sorrow.' Even the Buddha, it seems, was lost for words adequate to describe the ineffable. Nirvana, as Professor Stace has pointed out, is a paradox unreachable by the rational mind. It is the final solution of the eternal round of karma and rebirth, the latter a belief shared by early Christians for over five hundred years, only to be repudiated and anathematised by the Church at the Second Council of Constantinople in AD 553, which pre-ferred death followed by everlasting heaven or an eternal hell.

I do not believe in heaven or hell except in what people enjoy or suffer in their lifetime, or lifetimes. I cannot con-ceive of a divine principle condemning people to ever-lasting hell. Nor do I believe that anyone is totally evil. We are evil in parts and at different times but never the whole time. But I do believe that we are, to some extent, responsible for our actions, which involves, of course, a modicum of free-will. By our own acts we condemn our-selves. But condign sentence can only be carried out ade-quately by some sort of rebirth. One life is not enough to sort out rewards and retribution. What we make of this life determines what we must come to terms with in the next. In the end we get exactly what we deserve – no more, no less.

I do not, of course, *know* this. It is only a hunch. But it seems to me to provide a sort of justice which is difficult to fault and is not easy to accommodate in a linear, finite, black and white interpretation. No doubt readers will have other ideas. Quot homines – tot sententiae – and that again is as it should be. It would be a lot easier for instance to believe that after death there is nothing, a much less painful solution, since one would reach The

Void without having to work for it through life after life. But this would involve sidelining justice and since, to my mind, justice forms an important part of the final solution I find that difficult to accept. We can't wipe out the whole problem of ethics just because it is inconvenient and doesn't fit readily into our scheme of things. However, it is my opinion that whatever we conceive will be different from what comes to pass, though life's appearances may well present us with useful clues.

Claims that modern science is almost within reach of solving the 'riddle of the universe' are nonsense. We have barely scratched the surface. The psychologist and pragmatic philosopher William James has told us that our normal consciousness is only one special type. There are others all about it, potential forms of consciousness entirely different, separated from normal consciousness by the 'filmiest of screens'. We could go through life, and apparently most of us do, without suspecting their existence. Science is a necessary and useful tool within reason but it has its limits, and a meta-consciousness is apparently well outside such limits. The trouble with science is that for all its material successes it nevertheless tends to close minds to what doesn't fit in with its restricted field of enquiry. Scepticism should not be confined to what lies outside its 'cordon sanitaire' but applied equally within it. It could indeed be applied to normal consciousness which, in my view, presents appearances as the only realities, death as a final solution rather than a change of life, the Big Bang as the origin of everything rather than as a massive explosion, a super 'super nova' in a corner of a limitless universe without beginning or end. Proof? There is none, nor in this world can there ever be. I suggest that scientists have come to regard the Big Bang hypothesis as fact rather too soon and too confidently. The solution is by no means closed yet and there is still room for open minds. In life there are no final answers. Only questions.

Postscript: Since the Enlightenment and the materialism of the eighteenth and nineteenth centuries, openmindedness seems to have had a new lease of life. Scientists have been prepared to talk with mystics. The advent of quantum physics appears to have put some scientists at least in contact with oriental beliefs. Werner Heisenberg had consultations with the Bengali mystical poet Rabindranath Tagore. Erwin Schrödinger, author of the 'wave equation' in quantum theory, sought inspiration in The Upanishads. The physicist David Bohm, who had made a study of causality and chance and had written a revolutionary book on *Wholeness and the Implicate Order*, got in touch with Krishnamurti, had several sessions with him and together they published a series of dialogues under the title *The Ending of Time*. Fritjof Capra, another physicist, impressed by the similarities between Buddhist thought and post quantum science, published *The Tao of Physics*. Again, some Nobel prizewinners have apparently made use of the Chinese *Book of Changes*, the *I Ching*.

Such interplay between the rational and irrational has often proved fruitful. Leibniz, too, studied the *Book of Changes* as well as the number diagrams of the medieval Spanish mystic Ramon Lull. Newton studied both alchemy and astrology. Such combinations of reason and intuition or speculation have a long history. They were fundamental in the school of Pythagoras and have accompanied the pursuit of knowledge in succeeding centuries.

The Power Structure

There is a particular aspect of structure which applies to ideologies and 'isms'. Its culmination, or rather nadir, is totalitarianism, which includes everything within the structure. Such a framework provides a norm for the law-abiding, a prison for the dissident, a constraint for the over-adventurous and a support for the conventional. As an ideology totalitarianism is rigid, inflexible and harsh. It is embodied in laws, prohibitions, regulations, censorship, customs and controls of all kinds. It guides and ties the hands of the judiciary while empowering the military, police and prison service, as also other institutions concerned with correction and punishment.

In democratic or less totalitarian states the structure is less rigid and relates more to foundations, guides for procedure, buttresses against collapse, rites of passage, signposts for progress and benchmarks for orientation. Here police preserve the freedom of the individual rather than restrain it, and in courts of justice it is the civil law rather than the criminal law which is important. The indifference, fear, alienation and rejection of the individual in a totalitarian state is here replaced by a gravitational cohesion cemented by a recognised and freely adhered-to code of civility and behaviour. There are, of course, since there is more freedom, infringements of such codes but they are not part of the structure, which operates in a positive rather than negative manner. Unlike the structure of totalitarianism there is here the ability to bend and adjust both in space and time. In the totalitarian state both space and time are frozen, the whole being encased in ice.

The totalitarian structure has been graphically illustrated in an essay, 'The Power of the Powerless', by the Czech playwright Vaclav Havel. His model is Czechoslovakia under Soviet rule. He sees the pattern as a 'power structure' with an ideological base. The function

43

of the structure is to provide people, whether victims or pillars of the system, with the illusory belief that it is in harmony with both humanity and the world itself. It bridges the gap between regime and people, normalising their mutual intercourse, however difficult.

The ideology is a binding principle, a kind of glue, holding the structure together while at the same time providing rational support for it. The whole structure of totalitarian power, deprived of its glue, its binding element, would collapse and implode upon itself. The ideology is as essential to the structure as the latter is for the maintenance of the ideology. They prop each other up.

A roughly similar structure relates to another form of totalitarianism – global capitalism. Totalitarian communism enslaved one sixth of the world until the glue failed to hold. Global capitalism now threatens to enslave the whole world. Its masters here are not so much political tyrants or apparatchiks as tradesmen, tradesmen whose idea of trade is to buy up everything, including rival tradesmen, which they do with immense rapidity and efficiency and at the expense of the rest of the world. The difference here is that there seems to be very little binding glue but a lot of internecine cannibalism. The sharks are not only swallowing the minnows but each other also. The glue here is, of course, money, but money sunders as much as it binds.

In such a destructive and self-destructive structure not only the wealth but also the health, the ecology, of the planet is at risk. This is all the more sinister and difficult to combat as it is not yet recognised as totalitarianism. The face of communism was unmistakably obvious. The face of global capitalism is much less readily discerned. It is protean, hydra-headed, dissimulating, devious and well dressed. It has a smooth self-assurance which is at once disarming and inviting. We are half seduced by its sheer effrontery. Moreover it has not only us but governments themselves in fee. Its budget exceeds that of the majority of nations by incalculable millions. It has sucked the Third World dry and then piled a mountain of 'debt' on it in the name of 'aid'.

The structure of capitalism may appear less rigid than

that of totalitarian communism but it is more extensive and enveloping. If the structure of communism could be likened to a prison cage, that of capitalism could be compared with an immense octopus, its tentacles extending into every corner of existence. Like Laocoön, the priest of Apollo, who warned the Trojans against the Greeks and whose struggle in the coils of the serpent was immortalised in Lessing's statuary in the Vatican, mankind is similarly in the toils of the serpent of capitalism but, unlike Laocoön, does not fully recognise his constrictor.

How does one combat the octopus, the serpent, which has us by the throat? First one must recognise it for what it is, not what it claims to be, and this is not always immediately obvious since it has the advantages of wealth, the advertising fraternity, convention and apathy in its favour. Secondly it has a reluctant ally in nature itself. Our tyrant tradesmen cannot forever rob the world of its riches, its fossil fuels, metals, plants and ores. While nature may now supply the capital without which capitalism cannot exist, there are limits to its bounty, and plundering its resources cannot but bring exhaustion nearer. Thirdly nature itself is basically unpredictable. We cannot even predict the weather for more than a few days ahead. In the longer run, in years and epochs, nature's swings from hot to cold, from dry to wet, are perhaps predictable on average. If we are going through a 'yang' period now, we can reasonably anticipate a 'yin' period sometime in the future, but not *when* in the future. But nature does not confine itself to swings. Its changes may be extremely unexpected, dramatic and unpredictable. The structure becomes fractured and chancy, mirroring in quantum physics Heisenberg's principle of 'Indeterminacy' and in evolution the phenomenon of mutation. Such sudden changes may also be reflected in the environment in unpredictable earthquakes, floods, tornadoes, tsunamis, volcanic eruptions of the sort we have been witnessing recently world-wide.

This is no new phenomenon, however. There have been many such periods and more disastrous ones in the earth's history. The Great Ice Age was one example and 'The Flood' is another. There are many accounts of 'The Flood'.

In the Bible Noah's Ark finally landed up on Mt. Ararat. In Greek mythology The Flood was caused by Zeus. Deucalion was warned of it by his father Prometheus, who advised him to build a boat. When the flood subsided his boat landed on Mt. Parnassus. There are other 'flood' stories recorded by various nations. What was this flood? Could it have been the consequence of the end of the Ice Age? Or was it all just a tall story told at night around the tribal camp fire? The mysteries of myth are often unfathomable, yet even myths often appear to have a common structure recognisable over large areas of the earth.

That such events did occur, or could have occurred is strengthened by the evidence of tree rings. Recent tree ring calculation has focused on the year AD 540 and those immediately preceding and following it. Around the year 540 there appears to have been a major disaster affecting large areas of the planet – Ireland, Poland, Finland, Siberia, North America and even the southern part of South America. It is considered to have plunged people into 'the dark ages', with leaden skies, chilly summers, a succession of failed harvests and widespread famine. Up to a third of the people of Europe perished. The disasters have been attributed by a palaeoecologist to a possible cosmic catastrophe, probably a 'comet storm' in which the earth was bombarded by bits from the tail of a passing comet. Whatever the cause, something disastrous did happen. Ten years ago, in 1990, three British astronomers calculated that the earth had been seriously at risk of bombardment from a comet between the years AD 400 and AD 600.

Nature's structures, whether physical or temporal, are not rigid but, like others we have mentioned, subject to bending, to swing and rebound, and to fracture. Everywhere one detects an element of indeterminacy. This infringement of, and break with, regularity offers us hope. However imprisoned we may feel, our prison structure has the seed of freedom within it. The Dark Ages eventually gave way to the Renaissance. As Thomas Kuhn wrote in *The Structure of Scientific Revolutions*, science too has its paradigms, its patterns and structures which have to be bent or broken if science itself is not to ossify. 'Eureka' is the sound of a fracturing structure.

The Function of Form

'Form is both deeply material and highly spiritual. It cannot exist without material support; it cannot be properly expressed without invoking some supra-material principle ... . Form is never trivial or indifferent; it is the magic of the world.' – A. M. Dalcq., Professor of Human Anatomy and Embryology, Brussels

This seems to be echoing not only Plato and Aristotle but also Galen's 'dynamis diaplastike', Kepler's 'facultas formatrix', Paracelsus's 'Archaeus' and Goethe's 'Urpflanze' or original plant-form. The idea that growth was not haphazard but followed an ordered progression was the substance of Aristotle's 'entelechy' and his final cause in which growth sought an end and was drawn to grow by that end. The idea is by no means dead. It was revived by the world-known biologist and embryologist Hans Driesch, whose 'vitalism' was scorned by the materialists of the nineteenth century but which has been surreptitiously reintroduced in terms more acceptable to scientists and under another name in an attempt to account for the inadequacies of a mechanistic interpretation of neo-Darwinism. Philosophically it was taken up by Henri Bergson in his *L'Évolution Créatrice* where his 'élan vital' was the driving force of the 'facultas formatrix'. Literally it was the idea behind Bernard Shaw's *Man and Superman*. More recently certain biologists have diverged from the materialist path, notably C. H. Waddington and Rupert Sheldrake, so that the materialistic paradigm, which most biologists adhered to but is now under siege and battered by quantum theory, looks far less secure than it did.

Form, as we have seen, can be both static and dynamic, Platonic and Aristotelian. Form is the outer face of structure and the shape of function. It is the shape of the river bank and the form of the current of water that is con-

47

strained by the latter while at the same time eroding and altering it. Form infuses everything, gives shape to everything. It can be stretched out in time and, as Joseph Needham FRS tells us, regulates the development of limb-buds in vertebrates in successive stages, first anterior-posterior, then dorso-ventral and lastly medio-lateral. It is almost as though the body developed according to a certain rhythm, repetitious but also innovative. Professor Dalcq even calls the process 'morphochoresis', a *form-dance*. In embryology, he states, 'what is really primary is the mobilisation of the cellular elements, their arrangements in groups of distinct destiny, all in obedience to the severe rules of some ceremonious dance, typical for each type of creature'. He goes on to say that for neurogenically induced structures as for more simple aspects of morphochoresis the final result is 'a sort of Pythagoreanism'. A kind of knowledge is implied, of which an organism is not necessarily conscious, reminding one of Driesch's entelechy. The embryo differentiates, compares and evaluates both from intrinsic and extrinsic (environmental) factors.

In the writer's unorthodox way of crossing frontiers, trespassing and confounding disciplines, one is left with an impression of Jung's memory images (vererbte Erinnerungsbilder) and even of von Bertalanffy's 'systems theory' combining with evolution and historicism in a sort of morphochoresis, a formal dance, or music-score but capable of a number of individual interpretations on a variety of instruments and applicable in diverse fields. For, instance, as Joseph Needham points out, form is an essential constituent of organic chemistry and cannot be excluded from inorganic chemistry, nor indeed from nuclear physics. It is a necessary concomitant of experience in any field whatever. Form or structure (organisation) on the one hand and its dynamic counterpart function (energy) are two basic components required for understanding the universe, 'only with this background in mind can we hope to see how laws of each different level of organisation combine into a single structure – the natural living world'.

As an example of frontier crossing I have just come

across an essay in the current *New Statesman* (9.10.2000) by Mark Buchanan, illustrating a connection between physics and history – 'Earthquakes, forest fires and stock markets: do they follow a universal law? Can theoretical physics explain Labour's slump in the polls?' Apparently the author, who has just written a book, *Ubiquity, the Science of History*, thinks there may be such a law. There certainly seems to be some mathematical correlation but not, to my mind, a law. Buchanan calls it a 'power law'. Pressure apparently accumulates to a critical state in which everything becomes extremely unstable below the surface. Then at a certain unpredictable moment the whole thing collapses. The avalanche is precipitated, forest fires take hold, the stock market suddenly slumps, wars break out or governments are unexpectedly booted out by the electorate. The seriousness of the event is in inverse proportion to its frequency. An avalanche double the size of another is at the same time twice as rare. Similar ratios have, it seems, been discovered in earthquakes, mass extinctions and stock market crashes. In this light the structured historicism of Vico, Hegel and Toynbee looks a little less improbable. However, I find it difficult to regard this as a 'law'. But a tendency? I might settle for that.

This again is an example of the fracture of structures we have mentioned elsewhere. We can perhaps see an analogy in Thomas Kuhn's 'paradigm shift' in his *The Structure of Scientific Revolutions*. Such structure making and breaking seems to apply, loosely speaking, right across the board from field to field, from discipline to discipline from physics to geology, from biology to history. Not accurately, but loosely and approximately. Nature abhors accuracy. It leaves no room for diversion or development. It imprisons life. Here Heisenberg's 'uncertainty principle' seems to have got a foothold in the macrocosm. As in chaos theory we can never know precisely when the structure will collapse even though we aware of the build-up in tension. Something similar seems to occur in the process of radical discovery, a gradual build-up of tension followed by the sudden release at the 'Eureka moment'. As we have mentioned elsewhere, Eureka is the sound of a breaking structure or, on a larger scale, of a 'paradigm shift' – an avalanche of frozen structure.

This framework is penetrated ubiquitously by mathematics – approximation stretched on the rack of accuracy, for we cannot apparently make rational sense of things without measurement, however well sensation, feeling or intuition may serve us. Mathematics is the intermediary, the go-between, neutral, unsullied, ice-pure. As a go-between it unites the human mind with nature itself since both are seen to partake of it, as D'Arcy Thompson's *On Growth and Form* has made us well aware. Mathematics is not just a child of the human mind. It is the offspring of two parents, the mind and nature, seen as a unity, for we and our world are one. We are sewn into our world, part of it, as it is part of us. Mathematics is the visible part of the stitching, from Fibonacci to the Golden Section and the logarithmic spiral, to the musical scale, the colour spectrum and the curious relationships we have elsewhere displayed between the revolutions of the outer planets, 'the music of the spheres'. At the back of it all stand Pythagoras and his followers Plato and Aristotle, while more recently, joining in the formal dance, the morphochoresis, we have relativity, quantum mechanics and chaos theory, with chaos already seen as the womb of a new hidden order reflected in Mandelbrot 'fractals' or in Bohm's 'implicate order'. In the search for order both the human mind and nature itself are protagonists. The Greeks had a word for order – Cosmos. To Parmenides it was fixed; to Heraclitus it was in constant flux. Both were right, for the former related to the world of Being, the latter to the world of Becoming – our world of appearances or phenomena. The former is beyond our experience. The structure of the latter is in constant evolution.

Distance – the Anaesthetic of Pain, Responsibility and Concern

Distance is the interval between two points in time. It is a measure of function. Distance is also the interval between two points in space. It is a measure of structure. Distance brings us either closer to, or farther from, whatever we are observing, whether in space or time. If proximity is unpleasant, distance will lend enchantment to the view. This is particularly noticeable in war. In its early stage war was essentially fought at close quarters. To primitive man in the defence of his tribe or community the main weapon was probably the stick, the bludgeon or the spear. Later came the sword and the lance, all hand-held with the enemy at little more than arm's reach. As the weapon went in, the assailant could see what he was doing, see the blood spurting, the agony on his enemy's face. Even with the advent of the bow and arrow, although assailant and victim were further removed from each other, when the battle was over the dead and wounded were only too evident. With the sophisticated development of weaponry, however, such close contact became a rarity. One's enemy could be a mile away, a hundred miles or more than a thousand miles away. One could no longer see the results of one's actions. The primitive man might have felt elation or a few qualms of compassion. He might well have been related to his victim. Not nowadays. Feeling is no longer permissible, sight no longer possible except perhaps through a range-finder or long-range targeting instrument. When one fires a ballistic missile one does not have to come face to face with its consequences, with the rawness, the nakedness of primitive man. The remoteness protects us and our sensibilities from any unpleasant intimacy. Further to protect us we have invented an anaesthetic language to shield us from any pain or sensitivity that might leak through our prophylactic propaganda.

Whoever or whatever is at the receiving end of our bel-
ligerence is no longer killed, mutilated or shattered to bits;
he, or it, is clinically or surgically 'taken out'. It is all so
clean, scientific, clinical, emotionless, feelingless and
blank. We, tender souls, are spared the sight of shattered
homes, women and children blown to bits, a hospital
reduced to rubble probably euphemistically described as a
direct hit on an enemy stronghold or as 'collateral
damage'. Except in the sanitised form of television to
whose scenes of violence in fiction we have long grown
accustomed and inured, we are allowed little contact with
reality. Propaganda successfully masks what proximity
could not. It is now only the victims that really know
what war is about.

What is it in human nature that underlies such aggression? There is some basis for the claim that a certain
human type might be involved, a type which also often
appears to attain dominating positions in the lives of
people in any age. During the 1960s the Peace Research
Group of Des Moines USA did some research on
militarism. Over 2,000 people in North America were
interviewed individually on a scale of attitudes. Further
studies over the years up to 1976 produced the following
picture. Those scoring high on militarism tended to be
extrovert, misanthropic, neurotic, subject to greater discipline in childhood, socially irresponsible, egotistic and
conformist in their personal relations. They were also
likely to be dogmatic, intolerant, rigid, nationalist, racist,
patriotic, punitive, conservative, against social welfare and
for laissez-faire capitalism. It was suggested that an over
disciplined childhood led to misanthropy which in turn
led to authoritarianism, which led to conservatism and
nationalism, which led to militarism. This seems to be
oversimplifying a complex subject but, bearing in mind
that the Research Group itself was not without a modicum
of bias and probably found what it set out to find, there
nevertheless seems to be more than a scintilla of truth
here.

During the twentieth century militarism has had a field
day. Never before has so much been spent on the art of
mass killing. Exports of weapons of war are thriving. We

may not be able to feed ourselves properly but we certainly know how to kill; nor apparently do we blink an eyelid at the cost. Indeed it is a very profitable business. Britain is one of the major exporters of arms in the world, the others being the United States, Russia, China and France. These, rather ironically, are the permanent members of the United Nations Security Council. Armaments seem to attract to them an ethical code peculiarly their own. We as a nation are apparently prepared to sell to anyone who will buy for whatever nefarious purpose the buyer may have in mind. We have, for instance, frequently sold weaponry to governments who use them against their own people and, on several occasions, to our enemies using them against our own troops. People do not count. Money does. To say that arms manufacturers have made fortunes out of the blood of their compatriots could be, perhaps, an exaggeration, but it is not an obvious one. It may be a dirty trade but it is a very rewarding one for those who ply it.

Arms manufacturers and the governments that are their clients suffer from, or more likely enjoy, tunnel-vision. They see the product, admire its sophistication and efficiency, welcome the profit it brings in and then switch off. They don't want to know any more. The important thing is in their wallets and it is, of course, what they are there for. What the product is there for they would rather not know. They don't want to hear about people being gassed, shot, or blown to bits by their splendidly efficient, sophisticated, expensive product which they have gone to such trouble to perfect.

Distance can be seen as a sort of protective screen, almost an isolating structure. As Noam Chomsky points out in his book on the Vietnam War, *The Backroom Boys,* not only did the distance, several thousand miles, between Vietnam and the United States protect Americans at home from uncomfortable realities, but the official Pentagon Papers also distanced themselves from harsh truths both by omission and by the adoption of a clinical, sanitised, pseudo-scientific language calculated to reassure the anxieties of those who might question the rights and wrongs of what their armies were doing. In the Pentagon Papers there are, as Chomsky points out, 'no memoranda on bombs that tear the flesh with tiny arrows designed to cause maximum pain and impossible to extract without grave injury'. This is not seen as terrorism but as an 'efficient means of achieving American aims'. By defining the terror as a technical one, 'hard-headed and realistic', one can side-track any moral or compassionate considerations. Since it has been seen as a problem for experts it is a matter of physics, of cold science, not of human agony and terror. The children in hospital as a result might disagree but 'they probably don't understand the laws of physics either'. If, as Chomsky remarks, 'the backroom boys at Dow were forced to walk through the burn ward of a children's hospital, they might think twice about what they were doing in their laboratories'.

This is putting things into compartments, shutting out and shutting in, not making connections, especially uncomfortable ones. It is a negative facet of structures which are employed to twist content at the behest of form. It is a temptation of all holders of power to erect structures of conventional wisdom suitable for the carrying out of intentions regardless of truth. Such a structure was manifest in Nazi propaganda in the Second World War and has repeatedly been exhibited in the Gulf War and in Kosovo. It is employed by both sides and indeed all sides as a matter of faith, those who challenge the structure being denounced as traitorous or at least unpatriotic. Such protective but essentially false and misleading structures seem part of the 'software' of all wars or attempts at domination permeating life through media control or press censorship, whether open or tacit. Patterns of belief are imposed to serve purposes which pass all understanding.

Sometimes, however, the structural constraints are not enough to stifle freedom of opinion even in normally obedient or conventional populations. Eventually, for instance, younger elements of the American people revolted against the atrocities committed by their country in Vietnam. The banks of convention were no longer able to contain the flood of feeling and opinion which overflowed and breached them. The mounting cost of the war and the ever-receding prospect of victory also played their part. But structures have a habit of self-reconstruction when damaged. By the time of the Gulf War they were back in service again. We and the Iraquis were once more believing what our rulers and the majority of the press wanted us to believe.

A not infallible, but nevertheless common, indication of repressive structure is 'uniform'. If a structure has to be upheld by men in uniform then the structure is probably rotten. Uniform is an insult to free intelligence. It determines who is to be master, who servant. A salute is a gesture of subservience to dominance, unless it is freely given as a token of respect. A uniform may stiffen a weak structure but render a responsive one inflexible, laying it open to fracture. Uniforms sometimes take the form of city suits and ties, boardrooms, stocks and shares – a structure for power no less than an army and, since it is not seen as threatening, all the more dangerous. But the cast of mind corseted in the structure tends to follow a certain 'chreode', to use a biological term for a developmental path, for which the apposite adjectives are self-sufficient, self-serving and selfish. In the process of enriching itself it is bringing the Third World to its knees and in doing so rapidly destroying its own fundamental capital, the environment. It surfaces in multinational corporations whose gross income dwarfs that of many nations. It is a structure in which the limits of 'the bottom line' are ever expanding to infinity and, though it appears not to realise it, is in internecine war with the environment. It goes by the name of global capitalism. Which will emerge the victor – the globe or capitalism – is a moot point. At the speed we are moving it will have to be one or the other. We can't have both. They are mutually self-destructive. One of them has to give a little. Let those of us who are neither corseted nor favoured hope that the victor will be the globe.

It is not suggested that one take sides in a political show-down, nor puts forward the view that global communism would be any better. It might conceivably be even worse. It is not 'global' anything that is needed. It is the equitable functioning of part structures within wholes and of whole structures sustaining parts for the benefit of all. As

Gandhi said, 'the world has enough for everyone's need, but not for everyone's greed'. Environmentalists, Greenpeace, ecologists and Friends of the Earth are in the vanguard of a saner appreciation of our place in the world, how we are 'sewn into it' and how it reflects us. They are building a new structure, divising a fresh pattern for all to live by. With luck it may not be too late.

One's Need of Enemies

'It is internal opposition (in the same being) which makes external opposition (between different beings) possible.' – C. K. Ogden

Opposition is a function of the horizontal axis in Cassirer's vertical–horizontal cross. The most massive and all-embracing manifestation of opposition is war. It is difficult to wage war without an enemy. One needs opposition of some sort. If there is none then it must be manufactured. In the 'cold war' preceding and following the outbreak of hostilities in the Second World War first the Nazis and finally the Soviets were designated as the potential, if not the actual, enemy of the West. After the war the Soviet Union responded in kind, regarding its former allies against Hitler and especially the United States as potential enemies. This enabled both West and East to spend countless millions of dollars and roubles on armaments, espionage, nuclear and chemical weaponry and, of course, propaganda. Both sides now had an enemy without being at war. But since each was deemed to threaten war by the other, the armaments industry on both sides thrived mightily. With the collapse of the Soviet so-called 'communism', a totalitarian nightmare which bore little relation to previous forms of communism such as that of the early Christians, of the monasteries, of Thomas More's *Utopia*, or even of Karl Marx, the United States came to realise it had lost a valuable enemy. With the collapse of the Berlin Wall and the loss of Stalin's monstrosity Washington was in dire need of an enemy. Enemies are essential if only to project one's own misdeeds onto them. Without enemies one has to face them oneself. So a new enemy had to be found.

Castro's Cuba, though long regarded as an enemy by the pundits of the Pentagon and the White House, was too small and powerless to fill the role adequately, but there were other Central American states in the US backyard which could be seen as enemies threatening the most powerful nation in the world, and the more powerful one is, the more one needs enemies. Again one nation was not enough, but a number might meet the bill and there was a whole arc of them just south of Mexico, some of them with a dangerous left-wing orientation. The US backyard was under threat. One or two of these states were as close as five hundred miles from the frontline states of Texas and Florida. The enemy states included Nicaragua, El Salvador, Panama, Guatemala and Colombia, some of the poorest in the western hemisphere. Being poor they had elected left-wing governments in place of the right-wing regimes run by ruthless tyrants such as Somoza, whom Washington had willingly supported. Left-wing governments however were not acceptable to the United States, so, regardless of its responsibilities as a peace-keeping nation or of its obligations under international law, Washington sent in the CIA and trained right-wing guerrillas. In Nicaragua they were known as 'Contras'. They murdered over three thousand Nicaraguan children and teenagers and thousands more of their parents. In 1986, when the World Court condemned the United States for its unlawful use of force in Nicaragua, American representatives of the UN Security Council vetoed a resolution calling on governments to comply with international law. A similar history was the lot of El Salvador and Panama. In El Salvador more than 20,000 civilians were killed by death-squads related to 'security forces' trained by the United States. Earlier, in 1971, Chile had elected a socialist government. Chile was not in the US backyard. Indeed its capital Santiago was some four thousand miles from the nearest United States coastline. At that distance, one would have thought, scarcely a threat to the might of America. But a socialist government was seen as a threat. With CIA help and US money and propaganda, economic chaos was achieved, the elected government subverted and violently attacked, while the president, Salvador Allende, was assassinated (some say pushed to suicide). He was replaced by Washington's favourite, a ruthless

dictator by the name of Auguste Pinochet. General
Pinochet's rule resulted in the murder, torture or 'disappearance' of 130,000 Chileans, but the United States had
been saved from the dreadful threat of socialism.

With Latin American threats removed, Washington
could surely now sit back relieved that its backyard, even
its continent, was now safe. But it had done away with its
enemies and it needed a credible enemy. It was not long
before it found one – Islam and the Arab states of the
Middle East. Unlike the Latin American countries, many
of these were very rich indeed. Here the bone of con-
tention was not so much socialism but oil. The sheikhs
and ayatollahs were sitting on the richest and most extensive oilfields in the world. The first enemy was the Iran of
Ayatollah Khomeini. It was at war with the Iraq of
Saddam Hussein, so Washington proceeded to support
Saddam Hussein with armaments in the hope that he
would topple Ayatollah Khomeini. The Iran–Iraq war
came to an ignominious end with neither side winning an
outright victory but with great loss of life, largely peasant
or civilian, on both sides.

With the support of American arms and money,
together with the help of British armament firms supported by the government in Whitehall, Saddam Hussein
now turned his attention to the south, invading Kuwait
and threatening Saudi Arabia, both countries whose
ruling castes had been much-valued customers for armaments and Western technology supplied by America and
Britain. Moreover, Saudi Arabia was sitting on the largest
concentration of the planet's oil supplies. American vital
interests were at stake, and when these are concerned
America reserves the right to intervene worldwide regardless of any United Nations' ruling on the matter. Saddam
Hussein was no longer a friend but the enemy. The Gulf
War, initiated ostensibly to protect Kuwait and Saudi
Arabia from Hussein, was covertly a war to protect
American interests, the oilfields. An added bonus was the
genesis of an obvious enemy.

The war was one of the shortest ever recorded, but
during it 88,500 tons of bombs were dropped, the equivalent of several Hiroshimas, nearly two million people had

been made homeless, while the combined effect of the allied bombing and the subsequent sanctions was, according to the United Nations Food and Agriculture Organisation, the loss of 560,000 children. The war was won by the West, but could it be called a 'success'? With the vast loss of civilian life, the oilfields on fire and Saddam Hussein and his generals still left in power, it was surely rather less than a Pyrrhic victory.

It may be objected that we have here cast Western nations as the villains of the piece in common with Khomeini and Hussein. In a war there are inevitably villains on both sides and they are not so much their peoples as their governments. In this opposition of giants the poorest and weakest were sacrificed, while the rich and powerful survived. Sometimes the impression is given that war, or the threat of war, is not so much between equals but between the powerful and the powerless. On each side, whichever wins, the rich and powerful survive, the poor often lose everything. Wars may help the deprivers but they rarely help the deprived.

The United States has now been designated as 'Satan' by many Arabs, while Islamic countries of the Middle East are beginning to be recognised as the potential if not actual enemy of America, for we all seem to need enemies. Not so long ago a film *Siege* was shown in New York depicting a fictional invasion of the city by an Islamic power. Islamic residents of the city were, not unnaturally, horrified at the way in which the United States chose to represent them. This way, surely, madness lies, or at the very least a gigantic lack of responsibility. The average Arab, like the average American, is an unwitting pawn in the ambitious machinations of his government. He, his wife and children are seen as expendable not only to the West but often to his own rulers, and relentless propaganda sees to it that his mind is kept fettered and his eyes blindfolded. His rulers on the other hand, even if defeated, often manage to escape scot-free. War is a cynical game played by those who have, and yet want more. It is fought, however, mostly by those who have not and never will have, not on behalf of themselves but on behalf of those who use them to further their own ambitions.

The Perils of Belief

'Periculosus est credere et non credere.' Belief and non-belief are both dangerous. If it was true four hundred years ago when Jacobus Grandamicus uttered it, then it is surely as true now as it was then. The danger, however, did not apparently worry the Red Queen overmuch – 'Why, sometimes I've believed as many as six impossible things before breakfast.' Belief underpins structure and also undermines it. Belief, elusive as it is, is nevertheless essential. We cannot manage without it. Without a belief one is a slave to circumstance. It underpins one's whole life. It is not only the basis of religion but of science also, though scientists don't like to admit it. Their belief is that they don't believe. They either know, or don't know. However, they demonstrate belief with every move they make. What is a hypothesis but a temporary, prospective belief? But hypothesis sounds better to someone who does not believe in belief. Isaac Newton went further and denied that he made hypotheses. 'Hypotheses non fingo', he claimed in his *Principia*, a work by no means devoid of hypotheses.

To believe in someone is to trust them. We can't live without trust. We trust the milkman to deliver our milk, and he does. We trust the bus driver, the train driver, the pilot of our plane. If we didn't we would not travel much. We don't know that they will get us there safely but we believe that they will, and in 99 per cent of cases they do. Life without belief would be so restricted, so bereft of imagination, so petty and so narrow that it would be scarcely worth living. Imagine a life of certainty in which we knew exactly what the future held, in which there was no room for difference of opinion because we knew all there was to know. Since the future would be known there would be no point in trying to fashion it. There would be no point in anything. Knowledge is fine – up to a point. But beyond that we have to believe. Besides, as the history of knowledge has shown, knowledge keeps little better than fish. It has to be inspected from time to time to see if it is still good.

Our remote ancestors *knew* that the earth was flat and that the sun went round it. It was obvious. They could see it with their own eyes. It was only much later that their belief in commonsense had, they realised, betrayed them. Those eccentrics Aristarchus of Samos, Nicholas of Cusa and Copernicus had a hard time of it trying to persuade contemporary scientists that they were wrong. Copernicus was so scared of what his fellow scientists might say that he delayed publication of his revolutionary ideas until shortly before his death. It takes a long time for new belief to supplant the knowledge of centuries. It was over two hundred years before the majority of astronomers felt it safe enough to accept Copernicus. In the case of Aristarchus it was two thousand.

Now they have to accept Einstein, who claims that any point in the universe can be taken as its centre. Knowledge and belief have suffered yet another defeat and there are many more in store if science is to continue to expand. Take the Big Bang theory of the origin of the universe. It is now being accepted as true, a theory it is believed on the point of becoming a fact, the metamorphosis of belief into knowledge in the minds of those who should know better – scientists. The erstwhile Bishop of Meath and Archbishop of Armagh, James Ussher, who claimed that the world began in 4004 BC, was obviously of the same kidney. Do Stephen Hawking and our present cosmologists ever consider that they might be in the same bed as the good bishop? It is just possible, of course, that unlike the bishop, Hawking might be right but the universe, one suspects, is not going to founder, any more than it started, at Hawking's behest. No doubt there will be several more savants of the calibre of Aristarchus, Nicholas of Cusa, Copernicus, Einstein and Hawking, to say nothing of the Archbishop of Armagh, who will come up with other ideas. There is no finality, either of belief or knowledge. We are not on the point of discovering 'the riddle of the universe', as Ernst Haeckel put it, nor, I suggest, will we ever be. One of the certainties of science is that it is for ever being forced to correct its mistakes by those it has sceptically held at arm's length.

Belief erects for itself a credible structure to underpin it. Thus we have religions, philosophies, science and conventions to cover all aspects of existence. Such conventions and structures often appear at the time to be impregnable, but with the passage of events which do not correspond with, or cannot be explained by, the conventions, the latter are progressively undermined and may have to be jettisoned for they come to be seen no longer as a support but as a barrier to the further growth of knowledge. This is a painful process – the shattering of a firmly established paradigm – and is usually accomplished only with great reluctance. Eventually a new convention is established which will accommodate the events which the old established one had ceased to do. The process has been well described in Thomas Kuhn's *The Structure of Scientific Revolutions*. Often the 'paradign shift' takes an unconscionably long time, for the church and the scientific establishment are amongst its most obstinate obstructors.

Convention, a convenient cover-up for misplaced belief, is a barricade requiring courage to breach. Galileo and Copernicus found it so and even Einstein was assailed by scientists in Germany who set up societies to confute his theory of relativity. It could be said that they were right in that every new theory should be open to challenge, but their motive was more a defence of the old paradigm which they had grown up with and jibbed at changing since if the new were accepted they would have to rethink their whole conception of space-time. Most scientists are conventional people and hate their beliefs and revered 'laws' being overturned. Temperamentally they tend to be cautious and 'safe', and the passion, impetuosity and even 'recklessness' of genius is beyond them. When the impetuosity has broken the barriers and the recklessness proved to be fruitful, the new findings themselves become settled into a fresh convention and once again revered and defended. Any further discoveries, therefore, involve yet another breaking down of bastions and so it goes on.

The average scientist believes in what he can see, touch,

weigh, measure and in what accords with his reason. The genius, while accepting this, is prepared to stick his neck out and even to be taken for a fool. He risks going further, is sceptical of accepted belief and is prepared to believe if necessary in the unacceptable, to challenge convention and orthodoxy. It is a dangerous road to travel, for it more often leads to the crank than the genius. But if the risks had not been taken we should still probably all be 'flat-earthers'.

Our so-called real world is an apparent, 'phenomenal' world (phenomenal from the Greek *phaino* – to appear or show). It is a show-piece, a piece of theatre. The appearance is the result of our involvement in it. Just what it is an appearance of is hidden from us. My chair appears to me to be hard, capable of supporting my weight. It is coloured brown. It has a slight smell of wood and furniture polish. It is not static. It is growing older day by day, gradually disintegrating through age or the possible ravages of woodworm until the day when it no longer has the appearance of a chair. But without the contribution of human sense organs and intelligence its colour, its smell, even its duration, do not exist. It is I that collaborate with the molecules, atoms, particles and mostly empty space in constructing something solid to sit on, something which seems to me real and is indeed real to me because it is I who make it so. We are in a sort of double-bind with it all. We create our world and our world creates us. We stand or fall together. In a sense we and our world are one. For centuries, though philosophers might have understood it, scientists did not. Now quantum physics is making it plausible to all.

As we create our world we also create our own structures, frameworks for support, scaffolding for belief. Beliefs occur not only as a result of our involvement with our world and our experience of it, but they also help to determine experience. They select from the whole panoply of perception those matters which most interest us and are of most use to us. Usually if we don't believe something we are not inclined to probe further in that direction and so are unlikely to experience it to the full. Certain aspects of experience are then liable to neglect.

Take the case of colour as seen through the eyes of Newton and Goethe. Colours appear when light is passed through a prism. Newton's colour spectrum is composed of seven colours of the rainbow. Goethe's colour spectrum is composed of eight colours, adding the colour purple. Unlike Newton's linear range Goethe's is circular, purple filling the gap in the circle which, if visible, would be occupied by those wavelengths beyond the limits of Newton's spectrum, ultra-violet and infra-red, purple being a blend of violet and red. It is a circular, psychological spectrum. In Newton's spectrum there are no obvious opposites. In Goethe's version red is opposed to blue across the circle, orange is opposed to indigo, yellow to violet, green to purple. In Newton's spectrum there is linear progression according to wavelength. In Goethe's version there is the tension of opposites and their resolution. In his *Farbenlehre* Goethe wrote, 'The eye is forced into a kind of opposition by setting up the extreme against the extreme, the intermediate against the intermediate; it unites opposites in a common bond.' In 'Goethe and the Phenomenon of Colour' (in *The Anatomy of Knowledge*), Haltsmark writes: 'In Goethe's view colour is something undetermined and undeterminable, something that arises through the interplay of certain dynamic conditions and is moved in one direction or other according to the changing balance of the creative conditions. To see colour as the result of that dynamic interplay would be to see it within a pure phenomenon, an *Urphänomenon*.'

Goethe argued that colour was not a static quantity that could be measured and claimed that it was a matter of perception – it was psychological rather than physical. Goethe, like Newton, had experimented with a prism but had come to different conclusions. He decided that it was the interchange of light and shadow which caused colour. He used candles, mirrors, pencils, sunlight, moonlight, crystals and liquids. Whereas Newton was reductionist, Goethe was holistic. Newton's theory was more objective and therefore better suited to the rigorous conventions of physics whereas Goethe was trying to find some all-embracing explanation through perception and the psyche, i.e., subjectively. But we now know that in our phenomenal world there is no such thing as pure objectivity; any observation we make is unavoidably subjective. Recently the American physicist Mitchell Feigenbaum has claimed that Goethe's ideas had more 'true science' in them than Newton's. They were empirical and repeatable, as were Newton's. But what real scientific evidence was there for a quality of, say, redness which did not depend on our perception and that, inescapably, is subjective? Newton preceded Kant by some eighty-two years and had little encouragement to question objectivity. Goethe, however, was Kant's contemporary. We have, then, two colour theories, both apparently correct in their own terms, but one more subjective than the other. That of Goethe has been ignored. Newton's theory on the other hand is part of our heritage. Nevertheless Goethe had a strong supporter of his view in his younger contemporary Schopenhauer who, in his *Zur Farbenlehre,* had set out his own theory of chromatics. Can it be that we have missed something valuable?

We suffer from a craven obeisance to the claims of science. Together with consumerism it is now probably our prevalent religion. But the results of science are approximate and have to be corrected from generation to generation and century to century. As Alfred North Whitehead once remarked, 'Nothing is more curious than the self-satisfied dogmatism with which mankind at each period of its history cherishes the delusion of the finality of its existing modes of knowledge ... . This dogmatic common sense is the death of philosophic adventure.' The pat 'put-down' dear to many scientists – 'there is not a shred of evidence to support this or that', lacks the pertinent word 'yet'. Have we forgotten the thalidomide tragedy and the confident assertions concerning mad-cow disease? Perhaps we should remember this when we listen to the advocates of genetically modified food.

Science deals with only a partial aspect of reality. Omniscience is unattainable. There is no reason to suppose that what science ignores is less real than what it deals with. It could, indeed, be a bit incestuous. Terms of physics, for example, are defined in terms of one another. Scientists have built a ring fence around their profession (a temptation for all professions) and, like the Freemasons, few are let in or listened to who do not conform to the accepted conventions. Moreover, much of the rest of life, if not ignored or discounted, is subjected to the Procrustean bed that science has constructed in an attempt to measure the unmeasurable. There should be no 'no-go' areas for scepticism. It should not be limited to outsiders beyond the ring fence but applied equally rigorously to those within it.

Belief and disbelief are the accelerator and brake to everything we do, everything we can think of, even imagine. They are the springs and checks to life itself. When it comes to politics the scenario can reach frightening proportions. It can take form as war or peace, prosperity or starvation, the care or the abandonment of millions. Such vital questions are determined by people delegated by us to do so, governments. People themselves have little say. They are not educated to assess the issues and they are under constant propaganda to accept what their governments believe and these, in turn, are rarely better educated, or fitted, to judge such issues. In most cases it is a matter of the blind leading the blind. The led are led to believe their leaders and, in most cases, they do. In each country, when it appears, or is made to appear, that national sovereignty is threatened, the press and the media with few exceptions fall into line. The more acute the perceived crisis, the more 'patriotic' the response. Dissidents may be dismissed as cranks, labelled unpatriotic, or put under lock and key.

In war time, it appears, people can be persuaded to believe almost anything. The advice of sceptics – never believe anything until it is officially denied – though salutary, stands little chance against the official propaganda to which people are subjected. Governments believe what they want to believe, and what they want to believe is seldom the truth. It is rather what will give them an advantage over their opponents and is put out as propaganda. We all know this of course, yet most of us are so accustomed to it that we take it in with our breakfast cereal, even with the very air we breathe, without noticing. If we don't swallow it whole a lot of it goes down with the rest all the same. How else would people in all countries willingly sacrifice their lives and families for the ambitions of their power-hungry politicians and militarists? Belief can be a butcher. Hitler could not have got anywhere without the belief he swaddled in propaganda and from which he ensured that the German people could not escape.

Purpose – a Chicken and Egg Conundrum

Is there such a thing as purpose? Among scientists during the age of nineteenth- and twentieth-century materialism purpose was given a poor press. One could do without it. Purpose seemed to imply a purposer, which had in the past been an attribute of God. Since, in the scientific mind, God did not exist, neither did purpose. Even today that belief still lingers on among many scientists, perhaps the majority. Even if they can't deny purpose, for they all make use of it, many scientists have designed experiments to prove that the action of animals is not purposeful. As A. N. Whitehead has wickedly remarked: 'Scientists animated by the purpose of proving that they are purposeless constitute an interesting subject for study.'

Purpose is a close cousin of teleology, the doctrine of final causes that asserts that developments are due to purpose or design. The following is an example of teleology which many scientists may still find difficulty in accepting as such. In Jean-Henri Fabre's *Souvenirs Entomologiques* there is an account of certain wasps which can paralyse spiders, beetles and caterpillars with their sting, without killing them, in order to lay their eggs in them. The stinging is carried out so skilfully and accurately, and is so obviously adapted to the anatomy of the nervous system of its prey, with the aim of paralysing but not killing, that even a surgeon with a scientific knowledge of the animal's nervous system could do no better than the wasp does without any previous experience. The process of the operation is so unmistakably deliberate and objectively co-ordinated that it is quite impossible to explain as a chain-reflex, or as an accumulation of inherited experience. The paralysis is essential for the deposition of the eggs, but killing is out, for the eggs need to feed off the caterpillar. Such an example of teleology, of purpose, of means and ends cannot surely be written off in any way as pure chance.   The pattern and the design are over-whelming.

Related to teleology is Aristotle's 'entelechy', the apparently purposeful becoming actual of what is potential. Entelechy is a form of 'inner design', teleology of 'external design'.   Both Aristotle and in more recent times, Hegel, among others, insist that life is a process of design.   The difference between the two types of design is illustrated in the perennial question – which came first, the chicken or the egg? From an entelechy point of view the egg came first, its end or purpose being to become a chicken; the end is within itself.   From the teleological point of view, however, the chicken came first.   Its aim is to produce an egg; the end is outside itself.   In Jean-Henri Fabre's entomological investigations we surely have a meaningful collaboration of structure and function animated, if that is the word, by what can only be described as teleology or purpose.

The Mechanisation of Man

Do men long to become machines? Over forty years ago
Hannah Arendt in *The Human Condition* talked of a process
of biological mutation in which human bodies gradually
assumed shells of steel. From men's actions during the
last century and the beginning of this it would appear so.
Why do people stare at *Star Wars* films and Daleks unless
they are half infatuated with mechanical men? Feeling is
out; thinking is out; loving is out. They are all 'soft' or,
worse still, 'sentimental'. One must be hard, ruthless and
dogmatic and above all scientific, so what better model
than the man-machine. Scared at any suggestion of ten-
derness, man transforms his backbone into a protective
carapace with, hopefully, nothing that could be described
as 'soft' within it. The carapace is preferably of steel, hard
and impenetrable. Man's penis, promoter of life, becomes
a stick, a weapon, a hand-gun, a ballistic missile, a rocket,
even a nuclear bomb, a promoter of a million deaths. Is
man in love with violence and death? Look at the police
in their riot-gear. Are they not Daleks? Look at the army
with its uranium-tipped weapons, cluster bombs, land-
mines and nerve gases so designed that none shall escape.
This is not just science; it is the use to which science is put,
often to further a particular material aim, an anti-social,
arrogant, greedy and ruthless purpose. Human nature, it
is true, has always been prone to greed, arrogance and
ruthlessness but it has now become also the servant of science. The creator has now become the creature of his creation. Every new 'improvement' in death-dealing mecha-
nisms drags us all with it. We are puppets of mechanised
arrogance, trapped in a snare engineered by our own
devices.

This sinister entrapment threatens to spread to all fields
of human experience, indeed all the more rapidly since we
eagerly listen to and welcome the demands for more. And

there is a lot more to come, almost, we are told, everything. We are now apparently on the brink of turning the
most macabre themes of science fiction into fact – the
discovery of the potentials of the genome enabling us to
control, manipulate and change all forms of life and even
to clone and create new forms of life. We are back at the
controls, in the driving seat, with a map of the road before
us. The map goes only so far and is extremely intricate,
and the road has never been travelled before but we are
confident we shall find our way without mishap. The
other occupants of the car, however, are not so sure, but
are ridiculed as non-scientific laymen. This is a time for
experts. We forget that the experts are largely paid
employees of pharmaceutical companies and multinational firms eager to milk as much profit as possible from
our genes. As a result, information to the general public
will tend to be skewed in favour of such companies, the
virtues of genetic engineering emphasised and its dangers
underplayed.

Genetic engineering, whatever its consequences, is now
a fact. The crops with which nature has managed to feed
man for millennia can now be vastly and variously multiplied, animals may be improved out of all recognition,
new species or, if preferred, one animal, a single unit,
'cloned' – replicated a hundred, a thousand, even a million
times. But man, who can now create, change, improve
and destroy every living thing can now, of course, do the
same to humanity. Man has never been so God-like. An
incredibly exciting prospect. We will, it seems, be able to
do literally anything we want, cure incurable diseases,
perfect the human mind and body, make whole the halt,
the deaf and the blind, the autistic and mentally deficient,
or at least prevent them being born. We can feed the
starving millions, house the homeless, put an end to social
unrest and war. Maybe, who knows, we will be able to do
away with pain and suffering altogether and perhaps
prolong life indefinitely. Or so we have been given to
understand, not only by tabloids but by responsible
broadsheets also, with little or no hint of unfavourable
consequences.

Furthermore, it is not only the newspapers; scientists

themselves seem to have become infected by the hubristic hysteria. They appear to have forgotten that what they like to call fact has a nasty habit of proving to be fiction a generation or century later. If science is still to remain science it can only do so by subsequently correcting itself. We may think we know 'the secret of life' and forge ahead in this belief, only to find out later that we didn't quite know it all. We thought we knew about TB and had eradicated it. It is now coming back. We thought we had conquered malaria but last year West Nile mosquitoes even managed to invade New York, something they had never accomplished before. We thought we knew about antibiotics but these are often now useless since our enemy, 'Nature', has seen fit to fight back. Nature had its own immune system which we have cleverly managed to weaken through our own manufactured immunity pills. So now our bodies not only find it more difficult to protect themselves but our manufactured anti-biotics are also less effective. Have we so soon forgotten myxomatosis, the thalidomide tragedy, 'mad-cow' disease and Creuzfeldt-Jakob disease? The success of scientists in encouraging such aberrations and their failure in dealing adequately with them should surely give pause for reflection. Part of the trouble seems to be that we have mistaken science for technology. Science is about knowledge, technology about the manipulation of such knowledge. Unfortunately the servant now drives his master. Science is increasingly in the hands of technocrats who, in turn, are in the hands of big business. What should be a quest for knowledge is now largely subject to a quest for money.

Should we not then be a little sceptical of science and scientists? They confine their researches to certain fields of human experience and then pretend that that is all there is. But their fields are limited to the material, the rational, the sensible and the measurable, and much of human experience is beyond their reach. As Simone Weil has pointed out, they work rather incestuously in sterilised conditions rigorously observed, behind a ring fence impenetrable to the layman. Within this sanitised area there is knowledge, fact, empirical research and those rather less material disciplines reason and mathematics.

Beyond the limits of the ring fence there is a vast, largely unknown territory embracing the rest of human experience, the existence of much of which is denied or not admitted. Reason and mathematics are to some extent applicable to both the limited and unlimited territories and could perhaps form some sort of a bridge between them since they are not themselves material. But if science is considered, a priori, to embrace everything, as our gene-merchants appear to think, then there is no bridge and no need for one.

Science, however is not a 'tabula rasa'. It grew and continues to do so out of us. It should surely by now be obvious that 'homo sciens' is not a separate species from 'homo sapiens', the former being a specialised and restricted branch of the latter. Homo sciens is a child of homo sapiens, a precocious child who puts factual knowledge (sciens) above wisdom (sapiens), and now thinks it is on the point of knowing everything – at least about genes. The scepticism it trains on others is much less readily directed on itself.

The latest biological foray into the nature of the genome has presented us with a kind of logical circularity. We have scientists investigating genes which are in essence the potential past, present and future of other scientists. The investigating scientist too is not only the product of what he is investigating but its producer also. There is an incestuous quality about the whole set-up. He is in effect chasing his own tail, which seems to me a poor recipe for coming to objective conclusions. Moreover he acts as if quantum mechanics had never been heard of. Genes, after all, are material. Biology itself is dependent on physics. Cells are dependent on molecules, molecules and genes themselves on elements and the atoms of which they are composed. We can go further down the scale to particles, and particles, whatever they are – if they are – are not what one would call matter. Even the determinism that appears to go with matter has been undermined by Heisenberg's indeterminacy principle, which allows for an element of chance or choice. The materialism so cherished by genetic engineers rests on less firm ground than it would wish to claim. For anyone in want of a little authoritative scepticism in contrast to my own, might I suggest that he or she read Richard Lewontin's *It Ain't Necessarily So – The Dream of the Human Genome and other Illusions.*

In spite of its title, this is a seriously researched book. Lewontin is a professor of biology, a statistician and geneticist. In addition he reviews books on science for *The New York Review of Books.* Another sceptical source is Bryan Appleyard's *Brave New Worlds – Staying Human in the Genetic Future.* Both Lewontin's and Appleyard's books come as salutary douches of cold water to the overheated hype and wishful thinking of our tabloids and, regrettably, genetic engineers. And scepticism is no more necessary than now. Scientists once had a reputation for caution, but the selfish gene seems to have so bewitched them as to throw caution to the winds. We have been through a similar scenario with nuclear power. We thought we knew about nuclear reactors, which would produce cheap electricity. In fact the electricity was not cheap, nor were the reactors. Moreover we have had the monumental disasters of Chernobyl and Three Mile Island, countless dangerous leaks of nuclear fuel and now we are saddled with a host of out-of-date and potentially dangerous nuclear power stations which have to be expensively dismantled and capped. We never seem to have thought enough in advance about how to deal with nuclear waste, with uranium and plutonium active for thousands of years endangering our descendants for generations, perhaps even millennia. It may be that biologists are not as reckless as physicists, but once again we are dealing with a subject the ultimate effects of which are unknown and could well be disastrous. If there is a possibility of things going wrong, and there always is, then sometime, somewhere, it will go wrong. In genetic engineering the prospect of this happening could beggar description, for we are tampering with a formative function of life itself. Moreover we don't know enough. We think we do but our ignorance of the subject is monumental. Indeed, we have only just recently made its acquaintance. A further generation of research could perhaps insure against the worst mistakes, for indeed, one may be sure, there will be mistakes. But no, we want to rush in on a wave of Utopian credulity buoyed up by the prospect of fantastic cures for this or that intractable disease while at the same time discounting any adverse opinion. The intended ends are seen to justify premature and inadequately researched means.

'Gallia in tres partes divisa est.' Caesar might have said something similar about the partition of scientists as well as Gaul, though scientists seem to fall more easily into two parts than three. The difference became evident in attitudes toward the dropping of the atomic bomb at Hiroshima. Einstein, Leo Szilard and some others were horrified and against it, but the majority, and of course the technicians, military experts and politicians, were overjoyed. Einstein was especially mortified to see the results of his own work turned to such ends.

We have lived in the shadow of nuclear annihilation ever since. The Kennedy–Khruschev confrontation had the whole world on the brink of disaster; Nixon was only with difficulty persuaded from using nuclear bombs in Vietnam; and now the United States, prodded by the Pentagon, is trying to persuade us that it is in danger of nuclear attack and needs a version of nuclear 'Star Wars' to protect it. We are back in the MAD years, those of mutual self-destruction.

Nuclear power is not gene power but the latter could be just as threatening in the wrong hands and with similar ignorance. Moreover it is already in the wrong hands, those whose main aim is to make as much profit as they can out of it. It is they who are fuelling the lemming-like stampede to get on with it quick regardless of any unfavourable consequences that might ensue. And they are backed by scientists and a host of technicians. The fact that many of them are in the pay of big business, pharmaceutical companies and multinational concerns is kept in low key. True scientists are supposed to be free souls, not in hock to anyone. But this is what we call 'the real world' and in this world scientists can roughly be divided into two categories. There are those like Einstein and Szilard and a number of others who have the idea that science is, or should be, in service to humanity as a whole and that anything harmful to that end should not be proceeded with. Humanity must come first. There are others, and they may well be in the majority, who believe that there should be no restraints on science. Science is 'value-free'. If it can be done, do it. This is the credo of genetic manipulators and their backers. Unfortunately, in the past, this has paved the way for those scientific experiments in Auschwitz and the Gulag. Humanity must be in the service of science, not the other way round. A greater perversion could hardly be imagined. Yet that is the sort of scenario, embellished by humanitarian hype, that is being offered us. This ethical divide splits science in two. Strangely enough it appears to separate top scientists from time-servers and technicians. Among the former are those with ethical constraints – science is subservient to humanity. Among the latter are those who believe in an 'anything goes', 'value-free' concept of science – humanity is in the service of science. This is of course a crude division. There are some who do not fit easily into either camp, others who shift from side to side according to circumstance. Our rulers, whether political or financial, tend to listen more readily to the 'value-free' believers. After all, that is where the power lies, and without power little can be done. Should we not perhaps sometimes ask ourselves whether it needs to be done at all? It is not a panacea but something with largely unknown long-term effects. Gambling is exciting but science should be, surely, rather more than a gamble.

One may well ask how all this fits into a pattern. It is a pattern of thought, belief, convention and ignorance, of arrogance and self-service. It is also a series of partial patterns which do not recognise an overall pattern. It is divisive rather than co-operative, manipulative rather than understanding. It is a pattern which humanity's rulers have succeeded in imposing on the rest of humanity for centuries and has resulted in war, slavery, starvation, poverty and homelessness for countless people. This is not entirely due to the 'selfish gene'. Men are not programmed to be monsters. They choose to be. Equally we may choose not to be. It is this that faces us in considering our attitudes to genetic manipulation. We must not blunder into this as we have blundered in the past. There is too much at stake – possibly everything. And we do not know enough. Ignorance attempting to play God is a terrifying prospect.

Abstractions and Appearances

We have been talking of appearances and structures. Structures are appearances and appearances are structured. Structures only exist in our phenomenal, appearance world. One can see this if one considers quantum theory. In quantum physics potential becomes actual only in presence of an observer. Without an observer there is only potential. The observer *realises* the potential (Aristotle's 'potentia' or 'dynamis', Kant's 'noumenon'?). It is we, the observers, who bring our structured world into actuality. It is we who determine whether the fabled 'Schrödinger's Cat' is alive or dead. Without us the animal is mere potential, in a state of 'limbo', neither alive nor dead. It is we, in fact, who bring our world into existence, a world in which we ourselves are inescapably included. As Niels Bohr quirkily put it, our world is not only queerer than we think, it is queerer than we *can* think.

It is my view, though one I suspect not held by many others, that the speed of light is not a terminal constant. It can only be that in our anthropocentric phenomenal world. It is a useful construction of ours concocted by scientists to relate energy to matter in a manner which makes sense in the situation within which we exist and in which we have placed ourselves. We see the speed of light in Einstein's terms because this is the way our minds are conditioned to see it. Subject and object are bespoke tailored to fit each other. The construction works perfectly because it is designed to fit and cannot do anything but fit, as the science of physics amply demonstrates. But beyond our anthropocentric range of knowledge to which necessarily science is limited there are other worlds to which we are denied access since our minds and sensory-motor equipment are inevitably geared to phenomena, to appearances. Quantum physics has provided the first chink in the wall separating us from such other worlds. The chink leads to a bridge which we have not yet crossed and may never cross but I suspect that eventually we may. Such other worlds would of course be created and maintained by, and tailored to, other observers no doubt very different from ourselves and, perhaps, behind it all there may be an underlying primal 'Ground' – 'the Womb of all Becoming'. I suspect that if there is such a 'Ground', then, at that level, the speed of light can have no meaning. Light is instantaneous, the apparent speed being of our own manufacture. Similarly space then becomes an infinitesimal point, what Indian philosophy names 'Bindu'. Light does not go anywhere, space does not *extend*, while time has come full stop in Eternity. Becoming is resolved in Being. Everything is interconnected. All is One.

We seem to have intimations of this in quantum physics. Both the Einstein–Podolsky–Rosen experiment and Bell's theorem show that pairs of particles communicate faster than the speed of light, and change opposite spin instantaneously no matter how immense the distance between them. Bell's theorem is now thirty-nine years old and was verified in the Lawrence-Berkeley laboratory, California in 1972. It confirmed the possibility of instantaneity and the interconnectedness of phenomena at a distance. But like those scientists who refused to believe Copernicus for centuries, many apparently do not now wish to accept the findings since they conflict with conventional belief, and if no one does the observing, according to quantum physics what is not observed does not exist. Very convenient.

So what are our structures, our patterns that we have been discussing in various fields? Like ourselves they are 'the cloud-capped towers' in Shakespeare's *Tempest*, only there because they are observed, constructed by us, constructing us, guiding us, informing us, constraining us, directing us, imprisoning us, fictions in mutual commerce as are the interconnected patterns of our personal, social and phenomenal worlds. Just as we cannot exist without our worlds, so can we not exist without structures. Just as the spider spins her web to catch what she has to live on, so our minds construct structures to catch meaning. In our case, however, while they may inform, as does the web or 'internet', they may at the same time restrict, channel, conventionalise and ossify. We have to learn not only to construct patterns, but, if we are to break new ground, also to fracture our own constructions.

The down-to-earth reader may be mystified by our repeated emphasis on *appearances*. He wants to know about 'the real world', not appearances, the scientific world, not fiction. Unfortunately physicists do not deal directly with the real world but with abstractions from it – shadows, appearances. Their methodology is based on measurement. They cannot measure, weigh, calculate, time or estimate the speed, inertia or 'hardness' of most aspects of experience. They have little to say about colour except wavelength and frequency. Beauty escapes them. They cannot even measure wetness, let alone the St. Matthew Passion or even a sunset. Poetry is way beyond the reach of science.

Scientists can measure the force of an earthquake on the Richter scale but not the experience of it. An abstraction of an experience is no adequate record of the reality of such an event. It can explain how it happens in terms of measurement, stress, elemental forces and so on, but the sum total of these does not amount to an earthquake, which is individual, unique and qualified by innumerable mental, emotional and environmental factors. Many years ago the physicist professor Arthur Eddington remarked that science dealt with a closed world limited to the quantitive and measurable aspects of things, those aspects which scientific method feels competent to deal with. Other physicists such as Sir James Jeans and Werner Heisenberg have said the same thing. Moreover such abstractions are not necessarily out in the world at all. They may be just symbols constructed in the scientist's mind and perhaps, in certain cases, even peculiar to him. They are, in essence, shadows on the wall in Plato's 'Cave' in *The Republic*. The abstractions are taken for the real thing and applied as if they were universal and indisputable when in fact they are limited and tentative.

Let us hope those biologists intent on genetic manipulation realise their limitations. Life is more than the genome can ever know. One may analyse, interfere with and

manipulate the human gene. We may think we understand the gene, but the gene is only one aspect of life. It
may be the seed of life, but life is a lot more than biology
and if we think we understand the seed we cannot, in
spite of such prospective structures as we employ, determine the fruit. We just do not and cannot know what the
upshot will be. What is being so impetuously investigated
is also the well-spring of the investigator. We are examining our own actualities and potentialities and, as a
result, objectivity is a chimaera. Like the vicious circle or
the Ouroboros, we are swallowing our own tail.

Structures of Provocation and Interchange

We have talked of patterns or structures as frameworks for understanding, guides for thought, rules for conformity, boundaries for parts and frontiers for wholes. A structure may also act as a provocation, an obstacle to be surmounted. Karl Popper had the belief that the development of music depended on the structure, often dogmatic, of the canonisation of church music which led to the 'cantus firmus' (plainsong) against which such new departures as 'counterpoint' were developed. Here cantus firmus provided a provocative obstacle stiff with the authority of the church against which counterpoint could be seen to hurl itself. It was an invention in which a new freedom evolved while yet retaining law and order though of a new kind – a freedom without chaos.

In 1920 and 1921 respectively the German biologist Jakob von Uexküll published *Theoretische Biologie* (*Theoretical Biology*) and *Umwelt und Innenwelt der Tiere* (*The Outer and Inner Environment of Animals*) in which his ideas on the reciprocal commerce and interchange between animals and their environment were set out. He emphasised how each animal, through structure, skin and sensory-motor equipment, was adapted ('angepasst') to its environment. The idea was not entirely new, for it was to some extent foreshadowed in Friedrich Schelling's *Ideas for a Philosophy of Nature,* published over a century before. Schelling was known as the 'Wunderkind' of German Idealism and had as his mentors the neo-Platonists Giordano Bruno and the philosopher–poet Hölderlin with whom he was a student at Jena. Uexküll's biological theories can be seen as a sort of forerunner for a branch of what we have now come to know as the science of cybernetics. The following structure illustrates Uexküll's 'Funktionskreis' or functional cycle.

The Funktionskreis or functional cycle, anti-clockwise

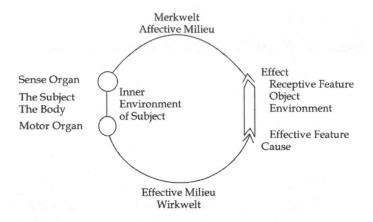

In animals instincts are also involved. In human beings the conscious mind cannot be ignored. Our bodies are part of our environment just as our environment is part of our minds. There is a constant interchange. It is not too great a step from here to those protagonists of cybernetics, Norbert Wiener and Ludwig von Bertalanffy, and from there through checks and balances such as bio-feedback and homoeostasis, carbon-dioxide exchange and global climate to J. E. Lovelock's concept of 'Gaia', the earth as a living creature. We and our world take in each other's washing and send it back just as the cell does, the body does, the mind does and the environment does. Life, as Heraclitus once said, is eternal change and the world, one might add, is, for better or worse, our changing room.

Five hundred years ago Pico della Mirandola wrote: 'Firstly there is the unity in things whereby each thing is at one with itself, consists of itself and coheres to itself. Secondly there is the unity whereby one creature is united with others and all parts of the world constitute one world.' Einstein followed him with: 'Without belief in the inner harmony of our world there would be no science', and A. N. Whitehead, in the same vein, claimed that 'All entities of factors in the universe are essentially relevant to each other's existence.'

Structures supply pattern to meaning, the grammar and syntax. But if there is an inner harmony and everything is relevant to everything else, then patterns should connect as well as separate. They must surely be fluid and permeable rather than rigid and watertight. They are elastic and approximate. To some extent they may be bent or twisted. In a sense they may be seen as 'alive'. They may also develop or evolve. In physics and chemistry they are more strait-laced, in biology less so. In human consciousness they leave still more room for manoeuvre, serving, in addition, as vehicles for concepts.

Structure is to function as river banks are to the flow of the river. They control and direct the function. In a philosophical sense structures leave room for both determinism and free-will. The determinism is in the origin and end of the function – in the broad direction of the flow, and its duration. Chance and free-will lie not in duration nor in origins or ends but in means, in the immediate contingencies of time, the actual flow at any moment. Since the present moment is always with us and the past and future never, we have at every moment a chance to exercise free-will in spite of the constraints of heredity, past upbringing, the need to survive, establish a career and the inevitably of death. We can at any moment we choose run off the lines, overflow the banks and even choose our own moment of death. The general flow of our lives may be broadly determined but its incidents are often ours to choose.

Patterns evolve. Biological evolution is pattern in progressive motion, pattern in the fourth dimension. Could the evolution of consciousness be similar? It is debatable that the present citizens of London are more intelligent than those of ancient Athens or the builders of the pyramids or even those who painted the walls of the caves of Lascaux. We may have more facts to play with, accumulated knowledge and technical expertise, but intelligence? I wonder. When one considers the man-made disasters, the wars, the cruelties, the genocides and the global manipulation of almost anything for profit and the continuing plunder of the planet's basic resources, the twentieth century has surely exceeded all centuries before it in the mindless, ruthless destruction and de-humanisation of mankind.

Patterns may sometimes be identified as 'fields' – electro-magnetic fields for instance, or other fields of force. Even in the 'psi-function' of extra-sensory perception and parapsychology a pattern, however vague, may often be traced.   According to the psychologist Jacques Lacan, the unconscious has a structure – 'L'inconscient est structuré comme un langage'. Noam Chomsky seems to go yet further in his claim that human beings are genetically structured with a language faculty. Where the top step in Plato's ladder relates to function, to movement, the lowest step relates to structure and form. Structure is the grammar and syntax of language while function relates to the utterance the voice, the phoneme, timbre and accent, the imprevision and instant exclamation.

Doubles and Counterparts

Everything has a 'double', and there are always at least two ways of interpreting anything, often as many ways as there are interpreters. The Delphic oracle was fork-tongued, its wisdom subtle and serpent-like. The oracle was female, a priestess of the 'Python', sometimes called the Pythoness. Her utterances were always 'delphic', two-way. Nothing was decisive. It was the petitioner who had to decide which way to take the serpent-wisdom and choice, of course, is double-edged. We like things single, simple and clear-cut, either black or white, not a dubious grey. But life and nature are neither black nor white. Like Jacob's coat, both are many-coloured. There are no straight answers, only hints, suggestions, hypotheses. As in Dante's *Inferno* we are in a dark wood in which lie hidden all manner of possibilities. We have, then, to approach things with our wits about us. Everything has its double contained within it, as Heraclitus, Hegel and Jung recognised. Even the human body is double. The male contains the female within it, and vice versa, even to the organs of differentiation, the sexual organs. This dou-bleness or duplicity is represented by homologues or simi-larities either in structure or in function or both. The male penis corresponds functionally with the female vagina, though structurally with the clitoris. The female uterus corresponds with the male prostate gland, the male testis with the female ovary. Sometimes what is large in one sex is much less so in the other, such as female and male breasts, or they can be external in the male, internal in the female, such as testes and ovaries. As in transsexuals, bodies may be virtually interchangeable and, through surgery, actually so. Male and female minds and emo-tions also complement each other just as their bodies do. Again, at times, one gets the male mind within the female body and the female within the male. In homosexuality the function is divorced from the structure both physically and psychologically. There is no complement, no completion of opposites, no 'harmony in contrariety'. Instead there is a quest not for 'the other' but for the same. In heterosexuality the need of each is satisfied by the contribution of the other, its opposite. It is assured of its own sex and needs its opposite to complete itself. In homosexuality there is often a lack of assurance in its own masculinity or femininity and further assurance is sought from his or her replica rather than opposite, in the presumption that like will strengthen like. But, as we have pointed out elsewhere, Eros is electromagnetic, not gravitational, and needs the coming together of like and unlike rather than like and like. It needs the 'harmony in contrariety' of plus and minus.

As a result of the inherent duality of everything, when we come to interpreting, investigating or judging anything it would appear appropriate not to take it at face value, singularly. Life not only has its opposite, death, coiled up within it ready to take over when its time has come; it has many other facets. When we have got over our inclination to 'look things in the face' it could be advantageous to go beyond the obvious and seek other view-points than the opposition, the acute or obtuse angle. It is a good rule, for instance, to turn what one is examining on its head, to look at it from the right side, then from the left, to compare the top with the bottom and, since there is an inner and an outer to everything, to turn it inside out. To discover any paradoxical property or eccentricity we should look at it askew and let the mind wander. We should look at it through a microscope as well as through a magnifying glass or telescope. We should see it as a part of a greater whole, or a whole containing many parts. We should look at it both as a 'loner' and as something unable to exist without multiple relationships. It might be helpful, too, to regard it as an outward sign of an inner meaning, or a meaning manifesting itself in a physical sign. Finally we should perhaps both believe in and doubt its very existence.

Public Means Private

One of the more obvious illustrations of a formative structure is an English public school. The tacit perversity of such a framework is evident in the word 'public'. A public school is emphatically not public. It is the most private of all schools. Among the more ancient of such institutions there may once have been some claim to the adjective but the public intended was that of the educated and moneyed classes watered down by the provision of places reserved for those less privileged, such as the sons of less than wealthy churchmen, for instance. Even the word 'ancient' was more often than not a misnomer brought in to add to their aura of learned antiquity. The great majority of so-called public schools are not in fact ancient at all, but built to educate the sons of the rising bourgeoisie in the nineteenth century – schools such as Radley, Marlborough, Cheltenham, Clifton and indeed the great majority. They were in no sense public though, copying Eton and Winchester, their ancestral and influential superiors, they adopted the word 'public' as a badge of acceptance as late-comers to the privileged hierarchy.

I myself was sent for seven stultifying years to one of these 'public' schools, a bastion, like the rest, of apartheid, snobbery, physical chastisement, slavery and petty hegemony. As a foretaste of prison it could hardly be bettered. In those days, in the 1920s, corporal punishment was the norm. The headmaster could beat anyone in the school. A housemaster could beat anyone in his house. Prefects and fag-masters were allowed to beat juniors. The fagging system, now thankfully outlawed, was in full swing. Teaching, however, though I never realised it at the time, was I suppose good, but snobbery dictated that masters were all Oxford or Cambridge graduates – no 'Redbrick'. I believe this has now changed and that girls are now allowed in, a belated concession which will surely do something to humanise a restrictive, authoritarian, unimaginative, almost fascist regime.

Mine was not a major public school but it is now some four hundred years old and should have known better, for it was founded when belief was beginning to come in for a few shocks. The future seemed to be about to open out. Galileo had his eye and his new telescope on Jupiter's moons. Shakespeare was writing *Othello* and *Measure for Measure* and had bought, two years earlier, 107 acres of farmland on the outskirts of Stratford. Galileo was teaching in the University of Padua and probably met my kinsman William Harvey who, after Gonville and Caius, Cambridge had gone to Padua, the foremost medical teaching centre in Europe. The University of Padua was broadminded and undergraduates were allowed to exercise control over their courses and elect their own teachers. This proved particularly attractive to students from England. Harvey, under the tutelage of the famous anatomist Girolamo Fabrizi D'Acquapendente, added to his Cambridge degree another from Padua. Back in England he began writing his *De Motu Cordis et Sanguinis in Animalibus*, the circulation of the blood, which was not, however, published until 1628.

Ideas were in spate. Doors and windows were opening. English public schools might have learned from the teaching regime of Padua but mine, and I suspect most others, apparently did not. It is interesting, and perhaps even educative, that Padua's liberal regime fostered the finest medical teaching centre in Europe. In England, however, we did not want to know and our public schools remain dedicated to not learning from the learning of others. It is time, for this and other reasons, that they should be replaced.

Language

The means we have of intercommunication, language, is unavoidably structured. We have mentioned Noam Chomsky and the French linguistic structuralists elsewhere. The structure of music has also been commented on in a reference to Karl Popper. We cannot express ourselves musically, literally or artistically unless we enlist structure of some sort, or perhaps a fracture or distortion of structure, or its denial. Cubism, Dadaism, Surrealism, atonic music or musique concrète are instances where conventional structure is seen as a provocation, a practice to be broken or a paradigm to be shattered.

The fracture of structure, of convention, evident in the writing of Marshall McLuhan's *The Medium is the Message* is described by Umberto Eco as 'cogito interruptus', or perhaps one might add in Eco's native tongue 'immaginazione staccata', and is viewed by the latter with evident distaste in an essay, 'De Consolatione Philosophiae'. In his essay Eco also refers to the French structuralists Roland Barthes and Michel Foucault, both linguistic iconoclasts engaged in the fracture of convention – structuralists engaged in deconstruction. In this case the 'cogito interruptus' is interwoven with 'joined-up thinking' in a way which opens up fresh vistas in the linguistic realm, however unsettling and disruptive the process may appear.

If we look at linguistics from a structural point of view we can relate it to the continuum structure–function observable in many fields. We have elsewhere considered this briefly in the field of physics. In linguistics structure relates to language, function to utterance. The former has a framework – grammar and syntax – the latter a function – a flow of speech. Metaphorically language is related to 'power', speech to 'force'. Michel Foucault claimed that power was everywhere while force was local and unstable. Power was a possession, a 'posse', a potentiality which can, or need not, be exercised. It was general. Force on the other hand was particular, for example individual speech. Without being exercised it had no meaning; its essence was in its application. Here language and speech may be related to physical structure and function and their mutual interaction. Just as structure informs function and function alters structure, so does language give form to speech and speech may in turn change the form of language.

A comparable process occurs in biological evolution in the interaction between heredity and environment in each of which structure and function co-operate in mutual self-modification. In the one the process may be predominantly entelechial; in the other teleological. In each version of the process there appears to be a latent capacity for radical change, an 'evolutio interrupta' possibly resulting in biological mutation. A comparable instance in psychology might be what Professor Allport calls 'saltatory becoming', a sudden unexpected switch of personality or behaviour due to latent capacities suddenly surfacing and taking over. In language the parallel is with new and revolutionary concepts such as those of Roland Barthes or Michel Foucault, some of the writing of Jorge Luis Borges or Joyce's *Finnegans Wake*.

In science a parallel mutation could be seen in Thomas Kuhn's 'paradigm shift' in which accepted structures of thought have come 'to a dead end' and a breakthrough into new patterns of thought becomes essential if further progress is to be made. More narrowly, structure, function and interruption may analogously be seen in an electrical wiring system or circuit. The power may be latent or active; the force, the current, is either active or non existent. The power electrifies the force, the force drains the power. Between them is the switch, the commutator which may switch on, switch off, alternate or shock. Seen as a structural rather than a functional system, the wiring is structure, the current function. The wiring directs the current but eventually the current may destroy the wiring which becomes faulty through over-use or being subjected to too strong a current. A parallel analogy is with the nervous system of the human body. Again the analogy is equally valid in the circulation of blood. Here the heart is the structure, the circulation the function. In addition we have not the cogito interruptus, nor the evolutio interrupta, but the circulatio interrupta, for the heart has its own brain, the 'sino-atrial node' situated in the wall of the right atrium of the heart. This node controls the rhythm and rate of heart-beat and is commonly known as the 'pacemaker'. The sino-atrial node is both switch and regulator. Its malfunctioning may result in heart-block or fibrillation. If the heart stops it may be restarted through electrical stimuli to the sino-atrial node.

In the mental field Eco's 'cogito interruptus', which he derides in McLuhan but nevertheless makes use of himself, is of great importance. At best it can provide the spark of paradox which logic lacks, at worst the flicker of paranoia (McLuhan?). Reason of itself is linear, predictable, the consequence being inherent in the premiss. Pure reason without the spark produces nothing radically new. It supplies the grinding hard work that precedes radical discovery but it is the cogito interruptus which finally brings it to light. It is the light switch, often found when one is most in the dark. It can appear in the most unlikely places, on the road to Damascus for instance or in Archimedes' bath, dreaming before a fire, riding on a bus or just putting one's shoes on.

Eco was surely right to dismiss McLuhan. Not every cogito interruptus is fruitful. The genius and the crank are sometimes close cousins but without the interruption, the breaking of the mould, the fracture of structure, the mind may stay imprisoned behind the time-honoured walls of convention. Without the sino-atrial node the heart would not function. In the nervous system, where two nerves synapse there is a small gap which electrical messages have to leap across. The functioning of two structures depends on a make-and-break interruption, sparking across a gap.

In spite of their ubiquity, then, structure and function cannot account for everything. There is a third factor – fracture coupled with breakthrough. The spark leaps the gap physically, mentally, in evolution (mutation), in science (paradigm shift), invention (new discovery), in religion (illumination or sudden conversion). So we now have not only the dichotomy structure/function, but also a triad, structure/fractured structure/breakthrough into new structure, coupled with function/interrupted function/breakthrough into new function.

Needless to say the above should not be taken too literally. Literal fundamentalism, like reductionism in science, channels the mind too narrowly and is not the best way of assessing organic life, which exists in virtue of approximation rather than of exactitude. I am aware that I have played fast and loose with analogy and even more with logic while using them as springboards for perhaps over-enthusiastic leaps in my attempt to interconnect what many would consider totally unrelated fields of experience. I can only refer the reader to these words of Pasteur: 'If someone tells me that in making these conclusions I have gone beyond the facts, I reply: "It is true that I have freely put myself among ideas which cannot rigorously be proved. That is my way of looking at things".'

Note: We have spoken of language as structure, speech as function. The function, however, may again be split into form (style) and content (the flow of meaning) – structure and function once again. Moreover, in Cassirer's vertical–horizontal framework speech could be seen as an occupant of the vertical axis since it is inherited and comes from within, writing as an occupant of the horizontal axis since it is learned, external and is not possible without recourse to material, environmental aids such as pen and paper. In general, structuralists seem to have given preference to speech over writing as being more original. The philosopher Jacques Derrida, on the other hand, makes a case for the written word in his claim that speech is a form of writing. But is not this just playing with words? Both, surely, have a common origin in what prompts meaningful gesture. Speech could perhaps be described as glossal gesture, writing as manual gesture, both functions again being subject to structure – tongue, palate and vocal cords on the one hand; fingers, pens and other instruments on the other.

Society in Disintegration

One aspect of structure is its liability to disintegration and fragmentation. The whole gets split into parts which isolate themselves and demarcate and follow a course of their own regardless of the whole. In society such compartmentalism can be recognised in class structure, apartheid, xenophobia, racialism, and narrow nationalism. It is largely the province of the comparatively well-off, the privileged sections of society, the self-sufficient, self-made and self-indulgent, but it extends also to those less well-off and poorly educated, especially where immigration, refugee status or the possible proximity of gypsies may be of concern, for such proximity, whether planned or not, almost invariably affects the underprivileged rather than the well-off. We do not have a class designated as 'Untouchables' but we often act as if we have.

On the whole, though, it is the poorer sections of society who have a better record of brotherhood, sisterhood and concern for others. Unless persuaded by the all-pervading selfishness of their 'betters' they tend to recognise, if not always act on it, that one is one's brother's keeper. If someone is in trouble, help, even in extremely difficult financial circumstances, is often generously forthcoming. Just after the Second World War my wife and I worked for thirteen years in the East India Dock Road area of London's East End. Inhabitants of the then borough of Poplar, bombed out of their homes and living in battered caravans, shacks and even tents on desolate bomb-sites, helped each other in a way difficult to imagine in an age in which one's religion is consumerism. Even today in poor areas competition is replaced by co-operation, greed and indifference by concern, individualism by altruism to a degree that one has learned not to credit.

In such cases the parts integrate with the whole. It comes down to the difference between treating another as an instrument for one's own advantage or profit and treating him or her as an end in him- or herself – as a whole, but also as part of a larger whole embracing all. It is also the difference between a hierarchical and a democratic society.

Compartmentalism is also one of the seeds of war. It sees others as alien, as French, German, American or Vietnamese, as Boches, Huns, or Gooks, rather than as human beings such as oneself, members, parts of an all-embracing whole. It nurtures factionalism, sectionalism, fundamentalism and, of course, cut-throat competition. Common good is sacrificed to private advantage. Fostering the growth of privatisation, it robs the whole for the benefit of a part. It is not only divisive but fundamentally destructive. It replaces love with hate, agreement with dissension. In spite of this it is what our rulers, almost without exception, support, for essentially it fosters their rule. In spite of our fantasising we have not a democratic society but an oligarchy. Precisely for this reason it will be difficult to alter, for we are all apparently in thrall to power. People have been brought up to see strong government as a virtue in spite of the fact that the stronger the government is, the weaker are its people. The last thing a strong people needs is a strong government, for they can govern themselves. Strong governments – let us recall some of them, Nazi Germany, Soviet Russia and China – are an expression of repression and tyranny. Regimentation, i.e., unity achieved through external force, is the enemy of integration, unity brought about by internal common aims and ideals and co-operation. Parts which do not integrate within the whole and go their own way regardless are like cancer cells. Modern society, fuelled by market forces and the drive for power, is fratricidally cancerous.

The trouble, however, is even more complicated, for market forces are not only at odds with the deprived; they are destroying the biosphere, bleeding the earth to death. Not only the biosphere but lithosphere and atmosphere are suffering its lethal embrace. If we cannot see that we are all in it together, that we must sink or swim together, and that what is preventing us from so seeing is personal greed and self-advancement at the expense of others, then we will all go down together. Pick-pocketing is of little account when the lifeboat is sinking. Those least aware of the danger are of course those who benefit from such ignorance. Even if they are aware, it is minimised, ridiculed or banished to the remote future. It will not happen within their lifetime. If need be, posterity can deal with it. It seems rarely of import that posterity will include their own grandchildren who will have a much more serious problem to deal with than their grandparents engineered and then proceeded to ignore.

One of the four horsemen of this impending Apocalypse is proving to be uncontrollable. Its name is unbridled capitalism and it is spurred on by greed and that glittering agent of materialist expansion, technology. We are already, as the cybernetic experts say, into unstoppable 'overdrive' and, bar a complete rethink and reinterpretation of what we are doing, where we are going and why, the impetus will take us all with it.

This scenario may never happen. Nature, in the long run, has a habit of rectifying the worst of man's follies but we are surely putting her needlessly to the test and this time it may well be too much for her. We have come a long way from the naming of parts and the consideration of wholes, from apartheid and comradeship, from class and classlessness, from division and unity. Why do we always seem to prefer parts to wholes, competition to co-operation, private gain to public service, egotism to altruism? Are the latter options in each case too difficult for us?

Parts and wholes are aspects of each other, being contained within and containing each other. In one sense they represent the inside-outness, outside-inness of things; in another sense the relationship between individual letter and the word which contains it, between the word and the sentence that contains it, between the sentence and its paragraph and so on to chapter and book. Without letters there is no word, without words no sentence. Each has meaning and its place in the general scheme. We live in a world which has decided that the letter is more important than the word, the word more important than the sentence, the part more important than the whole, the individual more important than society, private gain preferable to the public weal, national interests set against those of the rest of the world, in other words 'me first' regardless of others' needs.

If the origin of a whole is a part, then the end of a part is a whole. They are, or should be, integrated and mutually interacting. Isolate them, split part from whole and one is in trouble and if part tries to overcome whole; as with cells in the human body there is then ground for cancerous growth. We have such a cancer and it is growing rapidly.

Ensuring That The Future Has No Future: Genetic and Ecological Manipulation

In August 1999 there was a massive earthquake in north-west Turkey with thousands of lives lost. A day or two later there was another in the Caribbean. Again only a few days later there were further lethal aftershocks in Turkey, to be followed by another disastrous quake in Athens in which buildings toppled and hundreds were either killed or injured. Shortly after, in September, a devastating earthquake struck Taiwan. At 7.6 on the Richter scale it was more powerful than the Turkish quake and was followed by more than 1,000 aftershocks. So far it is known to have killed 1,712 people and injured more than 4,000, but the final count is certain to be much higher.

We live in dramatic times. This year (2000), there has been a record number of tornadoes, hurricanes, typhoons and tsunamis throughout the world, especially in North America, whose consequences have been great loss of life and much destruction. In retrospect perhaps this is nothing new. It has all happened before, if not in quite the same concentration. Those who survived have returned to the scene of disaster again and again. Is it that they like living dangerously, that it adds spice to their probably monotonous lives? One suspects not. It is accepted as part of the pattern of events of which they too form a part. It is normal for that part of the world.

But is it? For there are other quirks of nature which have not occurred for centuries, even thousands of years, and now appear increasingly threatening – the gaping hole in the ozone layer, the melting of the ice caps, the warming of the oceans, the pollution of air, rivers and land, the deforestation, the creation of deserts, the disappearance of bird, animal and plant life not restricted to any particular area of the globe but increasingly worldwide. It is not seasonal but permanent and steadily increasing. Unlike earthquakes and hurricanes over which we have no control, the warming of the oceans, the pollution of the atmosphere and the disappearance of species are man-made. By man, it is not of course meant the majority of people, who are sufferers rather than instigators of such global deprivation. The pollution, the 'green-house effect', is the result of the work of a minority of entrepreneurs in pursuit of profit and of those governments who support and harbour them, and most governments in a position to do so, do so. The planet is being exploited, bled white and perverted by a minority of powerful, unscrupulous people in pursuit of money. If there were no money in it, then, one could be sure, it would not happen. Plunderers are not accustomed to the idea of self-sacrifice. The snag is that through propaganda and advertisement they have persuaded many of their victims that what they are doing is sane, normal, good economics and of benefit to all. So we are all brought in on the despoliation of our very ground of existence, planet Earth.

What sort of structure is being abused here? It is surely that of Cassirer's horizontal axis, one pole of which represents the individual, the other the community. In a proper balance the needs of the individual should reflect those of the community while the community should respect those of the individual. In what we now refer to as the 'real world', however, the balance is markedly upset. The powerful individual considers himself of much greater value than the community. The balance is tilted away from the horizontal in his favour. The community barely counts. It is also an instance of the part considering itself more important than the whole and therefore entitled to rule the whole.

Basically this again is nothing new. The powerful have always dominated the weak but in the past it has been limited. Now, owing to the rapid growth of technology and communications, the domination is becoming worldwide. It might be an exaggeration to say that the whole world is at the mercy of such predators, but if little is done to halt their activities it will not be long before the exaggeration becomes a fact. Unelected, self-absorbed, avaricious manipulators are already in control of private budgets in excess of the national income of many states.

This increasing lack of balance is not just an ethical hiccup; it is a world-menacing material disaster in the making. Our planet depends on a framework of checks and balances to ensure its optimal function. This vital homoeostasis is now, owing to human intervention, ceasing to work properly. The feed-back is failing. It has gone into 'overdrive' and will, if nothing is done, self-destruct, bringing us all down with it. We have tilted Cassirer's horizon precipitously to such a degree that soon all chance of regaining equilibrium will have been lost. A main factor in this loss of balance is the perversion of man's relationship with his environment. In the days before the Industrial Revolution people took what they needed from the environment but also gave back to it. They ploughed and fallowed, sowed and reaped, manured and husbanded. They wooed the earth for what it could give them in return, the wherewithal for existence.

All that has now gone. Wooing is done with. It was too much hard work and too time-consuming. The new method is rape – the rape of the earth. Horses, which were kind to the earth and manured it, were too slow and were replaced by tractors, which compacted and tore at it. Rape is much quicker than foreplay and mutual enjoyment. It is also an expression of domination and power. The situation has been further aggravated by factory farms and 'agribusiness', by poisoning the earth with chemicals, by feeding cattle with hormones and injecting them with pharmaceuticals, by cramping chickens and other livestock into prison cages so small that they can barely turn round. In addition we have sprayed, waxed and primped fruit and vegetables to be nice to look at but tasteless rather than healthy and delicious, as if eating were a matter of eyes rather then of the tongue and stomach.

We have assumed that we could get away with it, that nature would not, indeed could not, fight back. We were mistaken. The virus disease myxomatosis, which we introduced to keep the rabbit population down, rebounded on us. Nature rapidly developed rabbits who were immune to myxomatosis. That was several years ago but we do not appear to have learned a thing. The thalidomide tragedy should have reminded us that nature was not to be trifled with, but after the first shock the whole episode has apparently been consigned to oblivion. More recently we have had salmonella poisoning, mad-cow disease and its human relative Creutzfeldt-Jakob disease, which has unfortunately proved fatal. We read now that Creutzfeldt-Jakob disease because of its lengthy incubation period could prove lethal to millions who have eaten beef as far back as the late 1980s – ten years ago.

Now we are to understand that malaria and tuberculosis, which we thought we had driven out worldwide, are on the way back. The malarial mosquito is now inhabiting temperate areas in which it was never active before. The city of New York has only recently had to be sprayed from the air by helicopters in view of the danger and New Yorkers have had to wear face-masks to protect themselves. It could be that London is next on the list. We know now that smoking may contribute to lung cancer but we still inject cancer-forming chemicals into the food we eat and, not surprisingly, the incidence of many forms of cancer is on the increase. Nature does not do this to us. We do it to nature. The spread of malaria to New York was no doubt the result of global warming for which homo sapiens, in his hubristic fantasies of power, dominance and avarice, is primarily responsible.

Not only is the whole being sacrificed to the part but the future is being consumed by the present. We give little thought to the sort of world our grandchildren will inherit from us. We must have everything now. The fact that millions in the Third World as a result of our rulers' greed have almost nothing now and will have even less in the future is not our prime concern, for we have been schooled to accept it. There are always winners and losers. In the over-simple code of commercial ethics the winners win because they deserve to, the losers lose for the same reason. The winners are crowned with the laurel of meritocracy, for merit means millions and the more millions you have, the greater the merit. The assessment of merit could not be easier. It is purely a matter of simple arithmetic starting with some six or seven figures before the decimal point.

We are now at the point when we, or rather our rulers, can decide whether to have a future at all. Once again. For we have been here before, with nuclear bombs which, with one exception, those who had them refrained from using. Now the number of nations having them has escalated and many more are scrambling to get their hands on the button to Armageddon. Possession of the means of world destruction is apparently seen as a badge of merit, as well as a dose of Viagra to an unfortunate state of impotence.

The problem of whether to have a future has now been ratcheted up again with the advent of genetically modified this, that or the other. At the moment it is being applied to crops and food but presumably it could be used on anything living, since every living thing has genes. Surely this beats even nerve gas, which, even if lethal, does not engender monsters. There are however two fatal attractions to genetic modification. The first, once again, is money and there is potentially all the money one could possibly want oozing out of the manipulation of genes. The second attraction is adventure into the unknown, for no one knows what the effects of genetic manipulation ultimately will be. There is no previous adequate model on which to base acceptance or refusal. This genetic casino, at whose baize table scientists eagerly sit clutching their infallible ciphers and betting systems, has been built and maintained by some of the richest entrepreneurs in the world. The scientists themselves are split. Those employed by the entrepreneurs think they know the answers and are eager to get going. Those not so employed, in view of the many imponderables, urge caution. No one knows how it will all end. Even nuclear scientists had a clue as to what would happen when the bomb exploded. We propose to entrust our genetic bomb to nature, for whatever we do with it nature is bound to have a hand in it – the gene is a part of nature itself. We do not seem to have learned much from nature. It could be that nature might resent our meddling with it yet again, and this time with the formative seed of its own existence. The broader scenario urges caution but the genetic manipulating firms, flushed with the anticipation of gargantuan profit and power, have already suborned governments in their support and legally protected themselves against libel and the attacks of sceptics unconvinced by their propaganda. Genetic manipulation is a much greater danger than myxomatosis. We need to work with nature, not try to twist it for our profit. One does not doubt the intelligence of the scientists or even that of their employers, but intelligence coupled with ignorance and irresponsibility is one of the most lethal combinations imaginable. Nature is a good mother but a bad servant and a worse master. It is time we recognised this before it is too late.

Star Struck

'If you believe in astrology you will attach importance to the assemblage of persons born under a certain planet; if you do not, you will regard such an assemblage as fictive. These distinctions are not logical; from a logical point of view, all assemblages of individuals are equally real or equally fictive.' – Bertrand Russell, *Human Knowledge. Its Scope and Limits*

To the more cautious the writer has no doubt stuck his neck out far enough already. He is now going to stick it out yet further. What is to come is not only not fully encompassed within the bounds of reason but goes beyond reason into the realm of paradox. Of all ostensibly unreasonable subjects astrology is probably one of the least respected. Indeed for an intelligent person to profess an interest in it is equivalent to intellectual suicide. Astrology is for the half-educated, the popular press and women's magazines – not, by any account, to be taken seriously, and certainly not by those who have a reputation to maintain.

Astrology, however, is the conceptual structure par excellence. It not only comprises Cassirer's meridian–horizon framework and Plato's 'elements' but also the 3 x 4 = 12 combination we have seen in Kant's 'categories' and the 4^3 of the genetic DNA molecule and Aristotle's syllogisms, together with the 12-sided dodecagon, the most perfect of the 'Platonic solids'. In its 'aspects' or planetary angles it provides us with a meaningful geometry and in its circles and spirals a cyclic progression through time. In addition it combines mathematics with chronology and symbolism.

This outmoded superstition has a very ancient history. It fathered the science of astronomy, or at least came to birth as the latter's less attractive sister. Every civilised country has, for good or ill, produced its own form of the art. For Westerners it surfaced as early as Empedocles and Plato. Plato's *Timaeus* is possibly the first astrological book in the history of Western civilisation. In addition it has provided the archetypes for much original discovery. Kepler, Copernicus, Galileo and Tycho Brahe all studied astrology while their detractors generally did not. Isaac Newton studied both astrology and alchemy. No doubt they had all read the *Timaeus*, perhaps the most fertile source book of ideas in the Renaissance. If astrology is what modern sophisticates take it to be after years of materialist indoctrination, how was it that men like Galileo fell for it? Agreed it was more popular then than now, but Galileo was not the sort of man to be taken in by popular nonsense. A more reasonable solution is that Kepler, Galileo, Copernicus and the like found in astrology an archetypal system of heuristic value. The Nobel physicist Wolfgang Pauli probably hit the nail on the head when in his *The Influence of Archetypal Ideas on the Scientific Theories of Kepler* he described such archetypes as 'image formers'. They provided the inquirer with a symbol system and 'symbols', as Paul Tillich has remarked, 'point beyond themselves to open up levels of the human mind of which we otherwise are not aware'.

This is, of course, a conception of astrology far removed from the popular, present-day obsession with fortune telling and the like which is as trivial as it is incestuous. To Plato the aim was always the 'megiston mathema', the greatest good. The chief narrator in the *Timaeus*, the man Timaeus himself, was a Pythagorean and here we see Plato infused with Pythagorean ideas. We could almost say this brings us right up to date for, as Ernst Cassirer has remarked, 'Quantum physics is in a sense the true Renaissance, the renovation and confirmation of the classical Pythagorean ideal ... . Science no longer speaks the language of common sense; it speaks Pythagorean language.' This, of course, is the language of astrology, and always has been.

The antipathy to the word 'astrology' so prevalent in academic circles today is emphasised by the fact that even that great Platonist, Professor A. E. Taylor, in his discussion of the *Timaeus* avoids the word as far as he can, yet the whole tenor of his argument concerns the meaning and form of the celestial 'arrangement' (cosmos), not its measurement. It is much more astrology than astronomy. The avoidance, however, is not just in name. It goes much deeper. Any scientist worthy of the name will surely examine his subject before pronouncing on it. Or will he? Not in the case of astrology. It is dismissed a priori as rubbish. He has not even bothered to distinguish astrology from the popular nonsense in the tabloid press. To him, very conveniently, that is all there is to it and, naturally, he is right to condemn it, an Aunt Sally only fit for destruction. Will he look further? Not if he can help it, and he has all the opinions of his colleagues to confirm his refusal. What, however, has gone overboard is scientific objectivity. He has jettisoned reason and empirical investigation for a priori prejudice which, of course, is exactly what he accuses those who don't agree with him of doing.

There have been, nevertheless, one or two serious attempts at research into astrology which have not passed entirely unnoticed. One was the work of the statistician Dr. Michel Gauquelin. After having recorded the birth times and places of thousands of celebrities, scientists, doctors, sportsmen, priests and others, Gauquelin discovered that there was a definite correlation between profession and planetary position at the time of birth, but it bore, in spite of its basic corroboration with the ground of astrology, little relation to traditional astrology and its current practice. Another research project was instituted by the psychologist Professor Hans Eysenck, one of the few academics to consider astrology at all. The result, however, was inconclusive. There was also considerable research undertaken by a group of academics and published under the title of *Recent Advances in Natal Astrology – A Critical Review 1900–1976*, a volume of some 600 pages, which was broadly in favour of astrology. At the moment there is a critical journal, *Correlation*, which attempts to subject astrology to reductionist methodology and technique. After fifteen years it has not been able to establish a convincing relationship between astrology and the world it is supposed to represent. This is surely a striking instance of the blindness of many investigators to the appropriateness of their methodology, for astrology is manifestly not susceptible to reductionism. The many factors of astrology form an integrated pattern, a 'Gestalt' form. They cannot be split up and isolated singly without falsification. They are integral parts of a closely interrelated whole. *Correlation*'s attempt to make astrology acceptable to scientists and respectable to the rest of us is, by restricting it to such methods, surely doomed to failure.

There is not much written in English to entice the serious researcher. Dane Rudhyar's *The Astrology of Personality* and John Addey's *Harmonics in Astrology* are among the best. In German, however, there is rather more. There is, for instance, Thomas Ring's *Astrologische Menschenkunde* (there is no English translation but roughly the title could be translated as *Astrological Anthropology*). It is a monumental work in four volumes with an introduction by Professor Dr. Hans Bender of the University of Freiburg. Another useful source is Dr. Freiherr von Klökler's *Grundlagen für die Astrologische Deutung* and, by the same author, *Astrologie als Erfahrungswissenschaft* (*Astrology as Empirical Science*), with a foreword by the internationally known biologist Professor Hans Driesch. Driesch was, of course a 'vitalist' and so generally dismissed by most mechanists and materialists. Finally there is the philosopher Count Hermann Keyserling, the founder of the Schule der Weisheit at Darmstadt, whose *Das Weltbild der Astrologie* is also pertinent. Unfortunately, to the writer's knowledge, the only English translation of any of the above is that of Keyserling and that too is almost certainly out of print.

The current dismissal of astrology in England no doubt owes something to ignorance of any serious writing in its defence as much as to the prevalent materialism of the eighteenth and nineteenth century. With the advent in the twentieth of relativity and quantum theory, in which materialism, if not yet dead, has received crippling blows, perhaps we may look forward to less material answers to our questions. Could it be that astrology is well placed to enter this new arena? If Ernst Cassirer is right in his philosophy of symbolic forms and science, since quantum physics now speaks Pythagorean language, the language, long derided of astrology, then perhaps there may be a foothold on the rock face of the scientific Olympus on which astrology might gain a secure purchase. Might? Could? Perhaps? As ever, the question remains open. And so it should be. Materialism tried to shut the door. Quantum physics forced it open again, open to a new world, a staggeringly complex and subtle universe in which there is certainly room for much of what the old world denied. An open door, an open mind. Let us keep them open.

What follows is perhaps a test of the reader's open-mindedness. Astrology is the attempt to discover meaning in the universe. That is indeed the basis of its structure and symbolism – universal meaning, Plato's 'megiston mathema'. It questions, as Pythagoras, Plato, Descartes, Kant and Hegel have questioned, that the universe is purely a matter of chance, without meaning or purpose, as scientists of the last two and a half centuries have tried, often successfully, to persuade us. It marks out the arena of a contest between order and disorder, design and accident, purpose and purposelessness. Modern science has come down firmly on the side of absence of design or purpose, especially in evolution. Astrology suggests that both design and accident play a part. If one studies astrology one cannot help coming to the conclusion that design must come into it. There is a mathematical accuracy in astrology which is difficult to dismiss. It links the birth of an individual to the cosmos through the solar system with a precision which is often quite startling. One can, moreover, through certain techniques, some of them unknown apparently even to professional astrologers, fine-tune the links between particular and general, real and ideal, in a quite extraordinary manner. Even if the individual link with development in time is discounted and the system regarded purely as a static, 'ideal' pattern, the combination of mathematics, geometry, logic and symbolism is a powerful basis for orienting mental exploration. It is of heuristic value if of nothing else. Galileo was familiar with his own horoscope but he also had an understanding of what lay behind it and how it related the individual to the cosmos. Goethe, too, knew his own birth chart and recognised its value. Kepler played about with astrology in his attempt to discover the laws of planetary motion and indeed paid tribute to its value. He made a number of miscalculations but his final conclusions are now part of the history of science.

Astrology is an exasperating subject. It is 'down to earth', centred on the rotation and revolution of the earth. It is logically coherent, consistent and mathematically verifiable. Yet at the same time it is host to a symbolism to which there is no limit. It is a challenging combination, at once a metaphor and a mathematico-symbolic system capable of providing signposts and clues which can assist not only those with enquiring minds but also those intent on breaking new ground. It is a tragedy that in the common mind it is unthinkingly dismissed as outworn nonsense. There are some things which are never outworn, whatever our current appreciation of them.

Astrology is a sort of marshalling yard for philosophical rail-tracks. It can accommodate lines running under many names and serving diverse routes and destinations. It is interesting and sometimes illuminating to relate it to, say, the ideas of Kant or Hegel, of Husserl or Merleau-Ponty or, indeed the writer's own preference, Alfred North Whitehead. Immediately a fresh view is generated. What had been previously understood takes on new meaning –'sub specie aeternitatis'. At the very least a stimulating exercise. The least amenable to such comparative exposition are positivist philosophies, but that one would expect. In existentialism the emphasis on immediacy, the particular and concrete as against the general and ideal, places it, in Cassirer's framework, on the horizontal axis the two poles of which accommodate Sartre's 'être pour soi' and 'être pour autrui'. Idealist philosophies, on the other hand, would tend to occupy the vertical axis.

In any field, theory is one thing, practice another. Let us take, for example, the confirmation of Einstein's theory of relativity. On 18 November 1915 Einstein received the news that an experiment concerning the perihelion of Mercury had verified his General Theory which, till then, had not been confirmed. He was overjoyed: 'I was beside myself with joyous excitement.' Now one can set up a chart for that moment and compare it with Einstein's natal horoscope. If the event is significant there should be close symbolic links between the two charts. At midday on 18 November the sun was at 25° 07' Scorpio opposing Einstein's natal Pluto in 24° 32 Taurus, a discrepancy of only 35 minutes. The Jupiter, Neptune and Pluto of the day in question were in close geometrical relationship ('aspect') with Einstein's natal Mercury. Symbolically Mercury stands for the rational intellect. The planet Uranus, on the day, was in close relationship with the mid-point between Einstein's Ascendant and Midheaven, i.e., the poles of the Horizon and Meridian which we have earlier discussed as Cassirer's framework for interpretation. The symbol Uranus has many meanings but among them are originality, invention, lightning intuition, as in Archimedes' cry of 'Eureka!'. Symbols may be interpreted singly or in combination. On the day in question Einstein's natal Ascendant was in close geometrical relationship with the midpoint of the combination Jupiter/Uranus/Pluto. This midpoint is reckoned by adding the precise degrees of each planet together and dividing by three and is a recognised astrological technique. In Reinhold Ebertin's *Combination of Stellar Influences*, which examines the meaning of symbolic combinations, one of the interpretations listed for this combination is 'the attainment of immense success'. Since the combination moves slowly it suggests a period of several days. However, it could hardly be more apposite. Moreover, all of the above contacts are within one degree of exactitude. If one applies the same technique to the discovery by Crick and Watson of the double helix and the DNA molecule the upshot is equally arresting.

All very well, one might say, but there were other people born on the same day and at approximately the same time as Einstein was, or Crick or Watson. It has been estimated that something like two people in five million have approximately the same horoscope, i.e., something in the neighbourhood of forty in Germany alone. What occurred to those others on 18 November 1915? The answer is not necessarily anything very much, for one must not forget that one is dealing with potentialities and those are not always, indeed rather rarely, realised. Einstein realised this – or rather the experiment concerning the eccentricities of the orbit of Mercury realised it for him, combining potentiality and actuality in a personal event of global significance, confirming his theory. It could be that others of his contemporaries also realized their potential but in a different manner. Planetary symbolism as a vehicle for concepts allows considerable latitude for interpretation. The planet Uranus, as indeed all others, has a large category of associated meanings. All we can say is that if something did materialise, to a contemporary its character would confom in *some apposite way* with the relevant symbolism of the moment.

No one has to take any of this on trust. The data are generally available and anyone so minded can repeat the experiment and confirm its validity. What is not susceptible to proof is the symbolism. This involves a measure of subjectivity which mathematics can dispense with. But then how far must one go to arrive at indisputable proof? If one reads Karl Popper it is quite unattainable, and one must be content with probabilities and approximations. In other words one must forego perfection for an approach to it, as near as one can. But surely this forms part of the meaning and thrust of life, the striving, the approach, not the arrival. The arrival is either perfection or death.

Sometimes the link between contemporaries, especially in comparable career, is remarkable. Pablo Casals and Lionel Tertis were born on the same day (29.12.1876). One was a world-famous exponent of the cello, the other a well-known virtuoso of the viola. The tenors Lauritz Melchior and Beniamino Gigli were also born on the same day (20.3.1890). A particularly interesting instance is that of two distinguished surgeons, Sir John Broadbent and Sir Comyns Berkeley. Both were born on the same day (16.10.1865). Both were married at the age of twenty-nine and at the same church. Both died on the same day (27.1.1946).

We can multiply such coincidences many times, and indeed there are countless such parallels, but they would still not provide proof, or rather enough proof. But surely they should invite enquiry. Coincident birthdates of unrelated people born on the same day of the same year are one thing. Coincident birthdates of related people born in different years are quite another. The record for the latter is surely held by Ralph and Carolyn Cummins of Clintwood, Virginia, USA. *The Guinness Book of Records* informs us that their five children were all born on 20 February, as follows: Catherine 20.2.1952, Carol 20.2.1953, Charles 20.2.1956, Claudia 20.2.1961 and Cecilia 20.2.1966. The book records that the odds against this happening are 17,797,577,730, i.e., almost four times the world's population.

We realise that we will never dent the armour of those determined never to shed it, but to the uncommitted, the enquiring and the open-minded there is surely food for thought here. In astrology time, place and event come together in significant coincidence, a coalescence which can be geometrically plotted, timed and symbolically interpreted. It relates the individual to his world as if sewn into it, or participating ('methexis') in it, a view in keeping not only with the geometry of Plato in the *Timaeus* but with post-atomic physics and philosophy since Kant. It is useless to look for certainty in astrology. Certainty is the Holy Grail of science and, except in mathematics, difficult of achievement. Astrology is more modest. Proof lies beyond it, not within it. It may point a finger but not establish an unshakeable handhold. It is perhaps more of a metaphor than anything. But it is more than the stage scenery of the play in which we are all actors. It embodies the meaning of the play.

Note: The philosophy of astrology has features in common with that of Hegel, and the application of Hegelian dialectic to an astrological chart can be very revealing. In his *Philosophie der Weltgeschichte* Hegel writes (my translation; I have no other English version to hand): 'Man is what he ought to be only through culture and upbringing. What he is on the instant is only the possibility of becoming what he should be, i.e., to be rationally free. He has only the disposition (die Bestimmung), the

obligation (das Sollen). Man must make himself what he
should be ... (G. W. F. Hegel, *The Philosophy of World
History*).

This is precisely the philosophy of astrology. A horoscope is a symbolic map, not of reality but of possibility.
Like mathematics, symbolism or logic, it is a mental construct. There is no material link with actuality, no mysterious influences emanating from the stars, no pseudo-
occult nonsense to delight the tabloid reader and give scientists an excuse for not considering it seriously and rub-
bishing it without investigation. Obviously it is anathema
to materialists but they should not, surely, jettison scientific objectivity to suit their prejudices. If they ask where it
all comes from, let them ask the same of mathematics. It is
all in the mind. Like mathematics it is an instrument for
informing us about our world but, unlike mathematics,
qualitatively rather than quantitatively. After relativity
and quantum physics, both about as 'immaterial', and the
latter as elusive as one can get, it is surely not such a pons
asinorum to cross. Scientists have managed to come to
terms with such intangibles as relativity and particles
which only potentially 'exist'. What appears to stop them
dead is that astrology is not seen as 'scientific' whereas the
intangibles of relativity and quantum physics are, even if
they overturned what scientists implicitly believed.
Astrology can expect no such happy U-turn in scientific
thought, for the bare thought that there might just be
something in it is unthinkable. It would present science
with a paradigm shift of immeasurable proportions. The
established religion must be defended at all costs, heretics
ridiculed and all those Galileos who believe in astrology,
as indeed Galileo did, should be put safely out of harm's
way. Increasingly science has become a discipline for
manipulation (tekhnē, technology etc.) rather than for
understanding (epistēmē, knowledge) which was its original function. Perhaps astrology could help to readjust the
balance. The use of the word astrology here does not, of
course, include the fortune-telling nonsense popularised
by the press and excoriated by scientists and academics.
There is a nucleus of researchers in Britain and other coun-

tries, notably Germany, who have done much to lay bare what this derided branch of symbolic logic has to offer. It is long overdue and its ramifications extend into all fields of experience. Most critics, however, seem to have no idea that anything other than popular astrology exists and would like to keep it that way. After all, why rock the boat? Science has had to forswear its findings repeatedly in the past and a paradigm shift of such magnitude as an acceptance of astrology might entail is a threat not to be taken lightly.

Afterthought – Astrology is a difficult subject to broach with those unwilling to listen, which includes the vast majority of scientists and academics. It has, however, met with a more welcome reception from psychologists and psychotherapists of the Jung school, for Jung himself became convinced of its merit in throwing fresh light on difficult cases of psychological interpretation. In a letter to Freud (12 June 1911) Jung wrote, 'My evenings are taken up very largely with astrology. I make horoscopic calculations in order to find a clue to the core of psychological truth. Some remarkable things have turned up which will certainly appear incredible to you ... .' Jung's friend, the late Dr. Gerhard Adler, a psychologist himself and part editor with Dr. Michael Fordham and Sir Herbert Read of Jung's collected works, also recognised the value of astrology and wrote a foreword to that effect for a book by Dr. Liz Greene, herself a Jungian psychotherapist.

I knew Gerhard Adler as a friend, not as a patient. Another academic so persuaded was a mathematician, the late Dr. James Williamsen, an American and Fellow of King's College Cambridge. He and I agreed to publish a book between us on the mathematical aspects of astrology – he had already published an aide-mémoire on the subject of 'harmonics' in astrology following on John Addey's *Harmonics in Astrology* which broke new ground in astrological research. Unfortunately our joint venture foundered due to Jim Williamsen's tragic and absurdly premature death at the age of forty-seven. I should say that I myself am not an astrologer, merely an interested and inquisitive amateur with a passion for enquiring into what Abraham Maslow termed 'the farther reaches of human nature'.

A Pattern Breaker – Simone Weil

Structures may make their impact on society as they do in the world. They also, in the form of laws, convention, codes of behaviour, tradition, habit and even fashion, control to some extent the way in which an individual faces others, takes his place in society and shapes his future. Most of us find it easier to fall in with the prevalent conventions of any particular place or period. We no doubt feel that if we did not, society might fall apart. But without the odd exception prepared to breach the rules, change would scarcely be possible. Structures would harden and further constrict. New ideas would rapidly be strangled by dogma and bigotry and the structure, instead of being a scaffolding for further development, would become a prison.

Happily, now and again, despite the pressures of orthodox opinion, accepted values and recognised norms, an individual gets born, lives and dies, as if navigating some frail craft, fighting against the current, managing to keep afloat, avoiding rocks and cataracts, directing a totally inadequate vessel towards ends which to most people would seem reckless and perverse if not mad. Such a one was Simone Weil, a French, Jewish, Catholic, anarcho-socialist, factory worker, trade unionist and intellectual. She taught Greek, philosophy and mathematics and in order to study Indian religion even taught herself Sanskrit. In addition she was a mystic whose writings were acclaimed by two popes. Few people can have lived such a dedicated, courageous and contradictory life.

She was born in 1909 in Paris, on the Boulevard de Strasbourg near the Gare de l'Est. She died in Ashford, Kent, aged thirty-four. Suppose we list a few of the inconsistencies which she turned into assets. Although Jewish by birth she was no believer in the Jewish religion. Her father, a doctor, was an atheist and even enjoyed telling

117

anti-Semitic jokes. Her mother, also Jewish by birth, was again no believer. Both parents were intelligent though not politically active. Her father had been an anarchist in his youth but in middle age confined himself to a well-meaning support for the socially deprived and dispossessed. Simone's brother André was a gifted mathematician. Simone herself was a brilliant student at the famous Lycée Henri Quatre, where among her fellow students were Jean-Paul Sartre, Maurice Schumann, later President de Gaulle's Foreign Minister, and the phenomenalist philosopher Merleau-Ponty. Maurice Schumann became a life-long friend. Rebellious by nature, Simone frequently broke non-smoking rules and also occasionally indulged in sports such as rugby which was almost unheard of among girls.

Intellectually ambitious, she set her heart on entering the prestigious École Normale Supérieure, the ultimate in French education. Simone de Beauvoir, later Sartre's partner, whom she knew, was also a candidate. In the entry examination of the two Simones, Weil came top of the list with de Beauvoir as runner-up. Her interests at the time were philosophy, Greek and mathematics. She aimed to become a teacher. She had, however, a gigantic social conscience and lost no time in joining left-wing movements. She was not half-hearted about it and went round with the communist paper *L'Humanité* sticking ostentatiously out of her pocket, but she never actually joined the party. She was much too much of an individualist and never toed the party line. When Franco invaded Spain with the intention of unseating the democratically elected socialist government, Simone was one of the first French to enlist on the government side and joined an anarchist battalion, only eventually to be invalided out.

Her dress often matched her character. She never cared what she looked like or what people thought of her and, although no beauty, she had a certain attractive strangeness about her. She was continually trying to harden herself physically, wearing no socks or stockings in winter and refusing to eat more than what she considered was available to the poor. She was short-sighted, awkward, and in manual work clumsy and slow. She had trouble with her hands, which were abnormally small. She also suffered from blinding headaches, but however ill she felt she always said straight out what was in her mind and her courage was extraordinary. Wanting to help the working classes, she decided to join them in their work. She became a member of a union and got a job in a firm making electrical machinery – manual work of course – she wanted the lowest form of work and got it. However, she was nearly sacked for her clumsiness. Later she was employed by the Renault car factory as a manual worker in their workshops at Boulogne-Billancourt, a suburb of Paris. She was no doubt a curiosity to the factory hands but she was accepted by them and she would spend hours instructing them in socialism.

After her period as a worker she reverted to her intellectual life teaching philosophy and Greek. Her thinking was much influenced by Plato, who became for her an almost reverential figure. Ever on a quest for truth, her socialism and philosophy, soon were followed by an interest in religion, especially in Catholicism, though she took an interest also in oriental religions such as Hinduism and Buddhism. It was, however, Christianity, which had absorbed so much of the thinking of Plato and Aristotle, that attracted her most. She regularly took advice from, and argued with, Catholic clergy and continued to do so until her death, though her independence, which had prevented her from signing on as a communist, also prevented her from being baptised and joining the church. She nevertheless began to experience mystical enlightenment, with Christ 'taking possession of her'. The conventional apparent dichotomy between communism and religion did not seem to bother her. The early Christians, after all, had been poor people and, following what they believed to be Christ's instructions, had adopted a form of communism later to be taken up by the monasteries, holding everything in common.

She began to write on Christian subjects. Pope John XXIII read her writings and was impressed. When, as Cardinal Roncalli, he had been Papal Nuncio in Paris, he called on Simone's father and asked if he could see her room. Typically it had a sleeping bag and no bed. He read her *La Connaissance Surnaturelle* and greatly admired it. His successor Pope Paul VI counted Simone as one of the three most important influences in his intellectual development.

When the Second World War broke out and the Germans invaded, the Weil family, being Jewish, moved for safety to Marseille. Simone joined the socialists there who were helping to support the French 'resistance'. She wanted, however, to be more active and to join the 'Free French', who were at the time operating from London. She somehow got to New York and from there back to London again. There she met her old friend Maurice Schumann and tried to persuade him to get the Free French to send her into occupied France in support of the resistance, known popularly as the 'maquis', a highly dangerous assignment with the likely possibility of death or torture, the more so in view of her Jewishness. However, her application was turned down. She was then living in Notting Hill, London and working for the Free French, but eventually her health rapidly deteriorated. She was taken to the Middlesex hospital with tuberculosis and shortly afterward died in hospital in Ashford, Kent.

A life such as Simone's would appear, in its originality, its contradictions, its idiosyncrasy and above all its singular paradox, its courage and self-sacrifice, to be utterly incapable of rational characterisation. She could be at once selfless and self-effacing, friendly but with a horror of intimate contact. She was known as 'la vierge rouge' but she was no prude, nor shocked by lewd language. She even persuaded a man friend of hers to take her into a Paris brothel dressed as a man as she wanted to see what went on there. They were both thrown out.

When one thinks of ideal rational structures or conventions to which people or events might tend broadly to conform, it might be as well, perhaps, to bear in mind the life of Simone Weil. Hers was surely a case in which the full force of the stream of function had breached and overflowed the constraining banks of structure, time and again. If anyone was atypical it was Simone Weil. She built her own structures and was a law unto herself.

(Most of the above information is owed to David McLellan's biography of Simone Weil, *Utopian Pessimist*, published by Macmillan, 1989.)

Is Science Credible?

Credo. I believe. But what do I believe? I believe in small things. I believe that if I wait long enough a bus or a train will arrive. But beyond that such beliefs that I have are largely provisional. To my mind there are almost no certainties except that the life I am now living I shall one day no longer live. However, I am not at all sure of what people call death. I have the feeling that what we call death is not an end but rather a change. Physics tells us that energy is indestructible though it may change from one form to another. I suspect that life is like energy. Heraclitus tells us that life and death are the same; the mortal is immortal, the immortal mortal. Euripides was of the same opinion.

I believe in the significance of metaphor. What we experience in our own life is a metaphor for something we are not yet equipped to experience. To my mind we are still trapped in Plato's 'Cave' in the *Republic*. We believe what we see, our world of appearances, to be all that there is and not the shadows or stage scenery that they really are. Reality lies outside the cave and we can't see it. Plato taught us that our world was merely an apparent one. The Greek word for appearances is 'phenomena' and it is our limited phenomenal world that science seeks to explore since, like the rest of us, it is still trapped in the cave.

As a consequence I have a number of disbeliefs. I am sceptical, for instance, about the present prevalent belief in The Big Bang theory and that the universe had a beginning and will also have an end. If there ever was a 'Big Bang', and there could well have been, it was not the beginning of everything; it was an interruption. To my mind the universe was there long before it. It was, is and will be always there. It was not born, nor will it die, though its appearance, since we are responsible for it, will die when we die or change with us. Our phenomenal world is unavoidably anthropocentric. This, it seems to me, is the meaning of Plato's 'Cave'. Stephen Hawking and the Hubble telescope are looking at appearances.

Metaphor tells me that as the day gives place to night and the seasons change and repeat from year to year, the annual rhythm is, as it were, a musical score for a celestial symphony embracing the whole phenomenal universe. There is not only a rhythm of the seasons but a rhythm of the sun and moon, of eclipses and celestial phenomena, for we are still talking about appearances. The universe breathes and pulsates. A Big Bang is only a cough, a change, not a birth of everything there is. Behind our phenomenal universe lies another, a 'noumenal', world as Kant called it. A world we cannot know unless we manage to struggle out of the cave into the light of reality, and even then probably not. To this world, the noumenal universe, there was no beginning, nor will there be an end, but perpetual change, the ground for the apparent change of the phenomenal world. We envisage our phenomenal world in terms of space and time since it is not immediately obvious that both space and time are the consequence of our anthropocentrism. We spin time and space out of us much as a spider spins its web and, having spun it, we get caught up in it for it structures our environment. We would indeed be lost without it.

According to Bertrand Russell, our bodies are actually parts of our immediate environment, an extension of ourselves into it. Jean-Paul Sartre claims that we are co-extensive with our world – 'sewn into it' so to speak – much as the old natural-philosophers used to think. We carry this immediate environment around with us for it is tied to our senses, being of course a structure of appearances. Our minds and sense-data are sensitive antennae presenting us with a picture of our world which we take to be real. Our sense of touch is limited to what our skin encounters, but our sense of smell has wider limits; our hearing reaches the thunder and our sight the stars. We are enmeshed in a network of sense-data linking ourselves to the stars, to the confines of our phenomenal universe.

What, one wonders, could lie behind the appearances?

According to the Copenhagen interpretation of quantum theory, Schrödinger's wave equation gestates a number of possibilities, of further worlds independent of each other. It is a theory which has been hotly debated among physicists and cosmologists and has been given the name of the 'Many Worlds Interpretation of Quantum Mechanics'. Such worlds would also appear to be appearance worlds. And yet again, behind these further appearances, could there not lurk a 'noumenal' world, in which there is no past, no future, no here, no there, only the eternal present and the ubiquitous 'here' – the Being, for which Becoming is merely stage scenery with Big Bangs perhaps occurring as part of the stage machinery? Perhaps one ought to re-read Prospero's speech in *The Tempest* (Act IV. Sc.2).

On the matter of appearance and reality concerning our daily intercourse with our world, I have been impressed by a passage written over a century ago by G. J. Romanes in his *Mind and Motion*.

If we unite in a higher synthesis the elements both of spiritualism and materialism, we obtain a product which satisfies every fact of feeling on the one hand, and of observation on the other. The manner in which this synthesis may be affected is perfectly simple. We have only to suppose that the antithesis between mind and motion – subject and object – is itself phenomenal or apparent: not absolute or real. We have only to suppose that the seeming duality is relative to our modes of apprehension, and therefore that any change taking place in mind, and any corresponding change taking place in the brain is really not two changes, but one change. When a violin is played upon we hear a musical sound, and at the same time we see a vibration of the strings. Relatively to our consciousness, therefore, we have here two sets of changes, which appear to be very different in kind, yet we know that in the absolute sense they are one and the same; we know that the diversity in consciousness is created only by the difference in our modes of perceiving the same event ... .

Does this not tell us something about the phenomenal

and noumenal universes? It does not, however, adequately explain why the former is assumed to be real, even absolute, while the latter is deemed not worth considering at all. We recognise a material event, but not what lies behind our perception of it, which is, is it not, its *fons et origo*, or if you prefer, its *primum mobile*?

Well, what does lie beyond appearances? Most scientists and all atheists would no doubt say – nothing. I used to be of that belief or persuasion myself. When some sixty years ago I read Darwin's *Origin of Species* I was immediately convinced. I became an atheist and *The Descent of Man* together with publications of The Rationalist Press compounded my conviction. What a relief that was. No more 'hell-fire', no feeling of responsibility, no come-back for any 'sins' I might have committed. I would just go out like a light and that was it. It was not until many years later that it began to dawn on me that perhaps such thinking was a little too easy, too comforting to be true. While I could not go along with the Church's idea of an afterlife which, nevertheless, did apparently depend, at least to some extent, on what one did in this life, the atheistic version seemed even more unlikely. Morality meant nothing. One could 'get away with it' and never have to pay for it. No wonder people were attracted to such a painless solution. Bertrand Russell appeared to think that facing total annihilation was an act of bravery. I would regard it as a welcome escape, for I can't get it out of my mind that ethics must play a part in the scheme of things. Though ethics is necessarily man-made, as is our world of appearances, it seems to play a not entirely worthless part in our experiences and to reach out to some Platonic ideal, however unattainable. Even in that atheistic religion Buddhism you don't get annihilation given you without a struggle, as our atheists seem to believe. You have to work for it through a series of rebirths. No easy escape there. But what finally brings you to the promised Nirvana? Is it not ethics? The way you behave in your lives among appearances? What one sows one reaps. To our nihilistic friends it doesn't matter what one sows, for the crop is destined for destruction anyway; one may sow tares and yet get away with it. Just because our apparent world is manifestly unjust it does not follow that justice is not something to be aimed at.

What, you may ask, has all this to do with Darwinism? Well, what has been termed neo-Darwinism seems to have persuaded some minds, including that of Professor Richard Dawkins of *Selfish Gene* fame, that anything other than annihilation is inconceivable. So it seemed to me in my youth, but I am a lot older now and a lot older than Richard Dawkins. It will be recognised that in the debate on neo-Darwinism I prefer the humour and mild eccentricity of his rival Professor Stephen Jay Gould to the inflexible arrogance of Richard Dawkins. Darwin provided us with a structure for the interpretation of evolution in our phenomenal world. It is not a closed book, whatever Richard Dawkins may say. There is still plenty of room for further versions which in a century or so may yet occupy the minds of neo-neo-Darwinists. We should heed Alfred North Whitehead. Each generation tends to think it has the answers or is on the point getting them. Science is continually having to correct itself of error, of having gone too far or not far enough and often down the wrong road. We never have complete answers, whatever we may think, and we never will. There is always, in everything, more to be discovered, and we shall without doubt know more about evolution. But we shall not know *all* about evolution.

I have no quarrel with science itself in its original sense of knowledge. The word comes from the Latin 'scio' to know, following on from the Greek 'epistēmē' which meant knowledge, understanding or wisdom. But science nowadays is only a particular kind of knowledge, a rather mean, reduced, sanitised version of knowledge, its high priests secluded largely in institutions or laboratories not open to those without the restricted brand of knowledge deemed acceptable to the authorities, a knowledge which dismisses all that cannot be counted, measured or weighed or otherwise rationally accounted for as unscientific. Within this sanitised parameter science has performed wonders and changed our phenomenal world out of all recognition, but while it has exceeded expectations in manipulation it has made little if any progress in understanding, especially in those vast areas of experience which lie outside its ring fence which, it appears, many scientists would like to reduce to little more than fantasy, imagination or myth. Even religion allows unbelievers into its sacred places, but unless one speaks the language of science and has degrees to prove it one won't get far in one's investigation into the hermetic, masonic world of modern science. The Ark of the Covenant of scientific knowledge is heavily protected.

Our world of appearances is an intricate structure. Apart from us, what keeps it going? A key instrument in keeping it up is time. As Hobbes, Richard Semon (*Die Mneme*), Cassirer and Bertrand Russell have noted, tactile sense-data, a necessary base for our phenomenal world, depend on time. Hobbes remarked that 'although some things are touched in a point they cannot be felt without the flowing of a point, that is to say without time, but to feel time requires memory'. Cassirer, following Hobbes, agreed that tactile sensation only arose through motion, which necessarily involves time. Semon in *Die Mneme* states that every stimulus leaves behind it a certain pattern, an 'engram', and each such structure takes part in how an organism will respond to future stimuli, i.e., the memory of the engram is crucial, which again, of course, involves time. Russell in *The Analysis of Mind* accepts mnemic causation, i.e., memory, as a cause of images but not of sensation. But is not the image itself an engram and thus a structure influencing future stimuli?

St. Augustine, whose thoughts on time are lapidary, made the point that expectation was just as necessary a concept as memory, again involving time, though in this case the future. Some modern psychology also stresses the importance of expectation, that one's view of the future as well as the imprint of the past partly determines our response to our world. G. A. Kelly's *Psychology of Personal Constructs* is an example. Again we see time and structure as necessary co-ordinates for our understanding of our place in nature.

There is one hypothesis that keeps poking its nose in here – that of teleology. Professor Hobhouse in his *Theory of Knowledge* states that teleology involves three elements –

a process in time resulting in some definite outcome, an element of value in that outcome, and the implication that the element is a determing factor in the process. We have remarked elsewhere that teleology is not a welcome possibility among many scientists today but it is difficult to explain that the world we undoubtedly experience all happens purely by accident. One can explain isolated, disconnected events by accident but co-ordinated, observable, rational, consequential events are not so easily dismissed. Why are they then so ingeniously interrelated and connected? Science interposes its veto – we must not ask why, for that would suggest purpose, would it not, and purpose is a Gorgon which scientists would rather not face. But if accident is only a partial, not a total, answer, then surely we must concede the possibility of teleology, that Plato and Aristotle may have been just as right concerning the integration of wholes as our present-day reductionists and specialists may be on the chance origin of parts.

For this and other reasons I tend to be somewhat sceptical of some of the claims of science. It seems to me that the natural-philosophers had a wider and more profound appreciation of knowledge, extending beyond measurement to meaning. I have a feeling that the 'why' is just as important as the 'how', the 'when' or the 'where'. I am, in the etymological sense of the word, an 'agnostic'. I have no answers, only questions. All I know is that I don't know, and everything I have said should be questioned. I have little doubt that if this is ever read, it will be. And so it should be. I cannot even say – 'credo ut intelligam'. Perhaps 'spero ut intelligam' would be nearer the mark. But hope is almost as perilous as belief.

Education

Our ideas and patterns of thought are structured by the type of education we have enjoyed or suffered. Such patterns change from place to place and from time to time. The history of institutionalised learning is a long one. We do not know much about the Egyptians, the Chaldeans, perhaps a little more about the Chinese, but in Europe we know that Oxford and Cambridge were preceded by the University of Paris, that Paris was preceded by Bologna, that some claim that the first university was Plato's Academy in Athens. Even that does not go back far enough. The School of Democritus in Abdera on the coast of Thrace, an area renowned for the stupidity of its inhabitants, anticipated Plato's Academy by a generation. If one doubts its claims to university status it should be noted that it dealt with the following subjects – Ethics, Natural Science, Mathematics, Music and Technical Works, which included Medicine, Agriculture, Drawing, Painting and Military Tactics. The section on Natural Science embraced Cosmology, Astronomy, Psychology, Sense Perception, Logic, World Order and the Planetary System. Abdera's only serious rival to the claim of earliest university is probably that of the Pythagorean School at Croton, which preceded that of Abdera by several years. Pythagoras taught his most advanced students separately, a foretaste of tuition at Oxford and Cambridge. The most advanced were known as 'mathematikoi', i.e., the learned ones. The rest were known as 'akousmatikoi', i.e., the listeners. He taught women equally with men and some of them became renowned. It took those upstart institutions Oxford and Cambridge some two thousand five hundred years to admit women on comparatively equal terms.

Although Croton was in southern Italy, it was not Italian. Almost the whole of the southern coast of Italy had been colonised by Greeks. Croton was a Greek city and Pythagoras himself was a Greek from the Aegean island of Samos. He was an Ionian. Ionia was one of the three early divisions of Hellas, the other two being the Achaean and Dorian. Ionia embraced not only the eastern islands of the Aegean and the coast of Asia Minor but also Attica and Athens itself. It was the most intellectual of the three areas. The island of Chios gave birth to Homer, Lesbos to Sappho. The city of Miletus fathered Thales, Anaximander, Anaximenes and Leucippus. Leucippus, Anaxagoras of Clazomenae and Epicurus of Samos laid the foundation of atomic theory taken up and developed by Democritus. Aristarchus of Samos claimed that the earth revolved around the sun while rotating on its own axis 1,800 years before Copernicus came to the same conclusion and put modern astronomy on its feet. Heraclitus of Ephesus fathered the doctrine of the tension of opposites and the running over of one into the other – 'enantiodromia'. It influenced C. G. Jung and laid the ground for the 'dialectic' later to be developed by Hegel and Marx. Heraclitus also developed a theory of perpetual change which impressed Plato. Finally we have Hippocrates of Cos. Ionians all. Can any other area, comparable with the size of Wales, have produced such a galaxy of genius?

The point here, in the theory of structure and function which underlies the view I am trying to express, is that from time to time in history there occurs both in space and in time a sort of 'knot' of events which bring together events of similar character, concentrates them into a potentially explosive mixture and then explodes, scattering its components sometimes worldwide. As evidence I would suggest the flowering of Greek culture and science and its intellectual brilliance, the Renaissance, the Enlightenment and the Industrial Revolution. It could be that we are now entering a technological communications revolution with the Internet in much the same way. Unfortunately the Internet, which informs but does not comprehend its information, provides us with millions of usually trivial 'facts' whose relevance to life we are not 'smart' enough to discriminate, and if we were smart enough, would suggest that the best way of interpreting its information would be financially, according to 'the bottom line'. If it did not meet the exigencies of profit it would not be worth pursuing. In such a revolution, in contrast to Ionia, we would be passive subjects of a Frankensteinian monster out of control, not free-thinking minds. A plethora of so-called facts has no relation to intelligence.

Goethe's 'Levity' and Nature's Numbers

There are four acknowledged forces of nature. In descending order of strength they are: strong (nuclear), electro-magnetic, weak (radioactive disintegration in beta decay) and lastly, gravity. It has been suggested by Goethe and more recently by Dr. Ernst Lehrs in his book *Man or Matter* that there is also a fifth force – 'levity'. To Goethe the growth of plants is not explained by the recognised four. Plants obeyed the law of gravity and fell to the ground when dead, but when they were alive they took the opposite course – upward. He concluded that whereas all dead or inanimate matter succumbed to the force of gravity, life itself tended to strive ever upward. Newton may have explained why his famous apple fell to the ground but he never specified how or why it got up there in the first place. Goethe came to the conclusion that the earth was surrounded by a field of force the opposite of gravity. Gravity was centripetal, drawing toward and centring on the earth's core. Levity was centrifugal, spreading upward from the earth's core and seeking the empyrean. The rising of sap in trees and the growth of plant life were assisted by such a force. While gravity drew down earthward, concentrating to a point, the earth's core, levity spread outward to a circumference, heavenward.

Science seems to have ignored this idea. Perhaps, like Goethe's colour theory, it seemed too bizarre even to deserve consideration and, if it is bypassed in textbooks, few people are likely ever to have heard of it. Indeed in a climate of narrowing reductionism it must, of course, virtually rule itself out. However, here, as the reader has by now recognised, we are dedicated at times to think the unthinkable. Suppose then that we entertain the idea for the moment, assigning it to certain poles of our vertical–horizontal diameters and comparing it with the electromagnetic force. If we follow the logic of vector-direction, the opposing couple levity–gravity should occupy the upper and lower poles of the vertical respectively. Here there is no one-way arrow of time but opposing lines of force. The centre of the cross is taken as the surface of the earth, the lower pole as the earth's core and the upper pole as the cosmic periphery. The lower pole is point-centred, the upper spread out. The former contracts, consolidates and dies; the latter expands, dilates and grows.

The electromagnetic force, on the other hand, could occupy the horizontal arm of the cross, its plus and minus, north and south, pulling and pushing in opposite directions. One could regard, as Dr. Lehrs appears to do, electricity as a positive form of magnetism, magnetism as a negative form of electricity so that the opposition and 'dialectic' is not only *between* the two poles but *within* each also. Lehrs appears also to link electromagnetism in, I find, a not too clear manner, with the opposing poles of levity and gravity. It would seem difficult to 'prove' anything of this. But we are not dealing with facts, of course, only with hypotheses and ideas. It does not matter whether it is true or false, only whether it is fertile and helpful in breaking new ground. As long as we recognise this, not much harm can come of it. After all, sometimes error can be more fertile than accuracy. Ideas such as these have not infrequently led to discovery even if the ideas themselves appear nonsensical. It is among the unusual, even the absurd, that new discoveries tend to lurk. Niels Bohr once remarked to Wolfgang Pauli that a new theory was not worth pursuing unless at first sight it seemed crazy.

To go back to our vertical. Suppose we consider the vertical–horizontal cross as denoting the influence of environment on a growing plant. Climbing above the horizontal we can locate the stem rising from the soil. Its growth is furthered by the elements. The upper pole of the vertical represents light and heat towards which the plant strives. The lower pole stands for the soil in which the plant roots and on which it feeds. On the poles of the horizon we have the elements air and water, air above the horizon,

water below it. We see here plant growth subject to the
four elements fire, air, earth and water, the four principles
or 'stoichaea', which Plato describes in the *Timaeus*, here
rendered geometrically as pointers for understanding, the
plant growth following the principle of levity.

We have been playing about with simple geometry and
number, using them as structures for suggesting possible
directions in which original thinking could develop. But
number pure and simple has often proved to be a springboard for discovery. Berzelius's estimate of atomic
weights was one example. Another, the Titius-Bode law
of planetary distances, is purely numerical. The discovery
of Balmer's 'ladder' of hydrogen spectrum frequencies
depended on the sequences 1.4.9.16.25.36 which are, of
course, the squares of 1.2.3.4.5 and 6. Then there is Pauli's
'exclusion principle' in quantum physics with its four
quantum numbers, and again Mendeleef's periodic table
of elements in which the octave played an important part.

Numbering is part of the mental equipment with which
we interpret our world. It is not a thing but a function, a
function out of which we erect structures for our understanding and manipulation. Elsewhere we have dealt
briefly with the numbers three, four and twelve. If we can
forgive a little Pythagorean thinking, three plus four need
a five to add up to twelve and $3^2 + 4^2 = 5^2$ give us
Pythagoras's theorem. Five is an astonishing number. We
have five fingers for counting. Five is the midpoint in the
series 1–9 and of the Pythagorean 'tetraktys', also of the
numbers on one's telephone dial. It divides into the 360
degree circle by 72, seventy-two degrees being an angle
whose significance was discovered by Kepler in his
Harmonices Mundi. Five was treasured by the
Pythagoreans since it was the midpoint in the ten-point
tetraktys, a figure regarded as sacred. As a fifth of the perfect circle (72°) it occurred in the five-pointed star, the pentagram which could neatly be inscribed within the circle.
Furthermore the sides of the pentagram cut each other in
the ratio of the Golden Section or Divine Proportion. The
pentagon was regarded as the Quinta Essentia, the quintessence of everything. It was related to one of the
Platonic or 'perfect solids', the dodecahedron or twelve-

sided solid, since each side of the dodecahedron was a pentagon. Since the dodecahedron was seen as representing the cosmos itself, it was, in theory, a pillar of the cosmos. If, as Galileo claimed, God geometrises, then the pentagram and its relations are splendid examples. The Pythagoreans regarded the pentagram as a symbol of health and it became the emblem of their community.

The ramifications of the number five and its derivatives are legion. As already mentioned, each leg of the isosceles triangles forming the pentagram is cut in the exact ratio of the Golden Section by the other legs. The Golden Section is found mathematically by the formula $(1+\sqrt{5})/2 = 1.618034 \dots$ and is usually abbreviated to phi (Φ). To Kepler this ratio was a 'precious jewel' and the Greeks regarded it as a ratio of rare beauty. The sculptor Phidias made use of it and the phi of the formula is attributed to him. The proportions of the Parthenon also relate to the Golden Section and in the Renaissance many architects, notably Andrea Palladio, employed it.

Connected with the Golden Secion is the Fibonacci Series in mathematics. Fibonacci (Filius Bonacci), otherwise known as Leonardo of Pisa, discovered the series and published it in 1202 in his book *Liber Abaci*, the book of the abacus or book of numbers. Each term of the series after the first two is the sum of the preceding two terms e.g., 1.1.2.3.5.8.13.21.34.55 and so on. The connection with the Golden Section is this. If we take one number and divide it by its preceding number we get phi (Φ) or very near it, $55/34 = 1.6176$ for example, but if we take higher numbers we get nearer and nearer still, but never quite reach it exactly, for instance $144/89 = 1.6179$ and $233/144$ 1.6180. Here again we have the natural inexactitude we have mentioned elsewhere. This series crops up over and over again in nature, relating mind to matter in an uncanny way.

Connected with both the Section and the Series is the logarithmic spiral or Spira Mirabilis. This relates to the Series in that the Fibonacci numbers, with their regular growth increase, can be plotted on squared paper to form a logarithmic spiral. Life develops approximately according to a logarithmic growth. The period of

menstruation is approximately 28 days or one lunar
month. Birth on average is 280 days or ten lunar months
(9 calendar months) after conception. Childhood ends
with 2,800 days or 100 lunar months, i.e. 7.7 years, followed by adolescence, maturity and old, age lasting 28,000
days, 1,000 lunar months or 77.7 years. The figures, of
course, are approximate and average. It appears, nevertheless, as an index of the speed of entelechy in physical
development – very rapid in the embryo, less so in childhood and very much slowed down in old age and is an
explanation of why when one is a child time seems to drag
interminably and yet races by when we are old.

The logarithmic spiral appears to have a relationship,
through Fechner's law, with the way we interpret our
world through our five senses (the number five again).
The German psychologist Fechner found that the response
to a stimulus was proportional to the log of the stimulus,
so that we can draw an exponential spiral to illustrate the
proportional sensitivity of eye and ear to the increase or
decrease of the stimulus. Fechner's law is not exact for
stimulus/response in all circumstances but it is a useful
working rule.

In zoology also the Spira Mirabilis plays a notable part.
It seems to have some relation to growth, the horns, beaks,
claws and tusks of animals being conspicuous examples.
The shell of the *Nautilus* is an almost perfect logarithmic
curve and as it develops the growth continues to follow
the logarithmic curve. In botany flowers such as the
daisy, sunflower and aster have centres made up of florets
arranged in intersecting logarithmic spirals. In the daisy
family the numbers of ray-florets also correspond to the
Fibonacci Series. In the sunflower head the series and the
spiral are combined. In his book *On Growth and Form*,
D'Arcy Thompson describes the spiralling of shoots up
the stems of plants: 'the successive shoots or successive
increments of growth, are tangents to a curve, and this
curve is a true logarithmic spiral.'

The Fibonacci Series and the Spira Mirabilis are again
combined in the semitones of the chromatic scale in music.
The Series is related to the sequence of white and black
notes on the piano keyboard and to the distance between

the frets of a guitar. A curious discovery is that Fibonacci also relates to the heredity of the drone bee. The drone has a mother but no father and so has five great-great-grandparents. The parents of these great-great-grandparents are eight in number, so that we now have 5 – 8 – 13, thirteen being the number of all the ancestors grandparents while five, eight and thirteen are all Fibonacci numbers. This ubiquitous series crops up again in the breeding of rabbits. Just how it does so is too complicated to set out here, but those interested will find an explanation in *The Divine Proportion* by H. E. Huntley (Dover, New York, 1970). Finally we can go to the limits of magnitude and still find traces of this strange pair. The galaxies and spiral nebulae correspond in shape to the logarithmic spiral while, at the other extreme, the Fibonacci Series appears in the histories of an atomic electron.

A circle is a closed, perfect, repetitious figure. A spiral, on the other hand, is an open, imperfect, incremental figure. A circle does not grow, a spiral does. Unlike the circle it is not final. It expands and grows in space-time. If the circle is a symbol of Being, the spiral is a means of Becoming. It demonstrates the effect of function on structure. Whereas function is an accelerated form of structure, the latter is a slowed-down form of function. This can be seen in human anatomy (structure) and physiology (function), where just as bone may determine the extent of muscle action, so the latter in the course of time will change, however slightly, the conformation of bone, for the spiral is also an exemplification of time. It is teleological and carries with it the ideas of intention and purpose. The sunflower head and the spiral nebulae are not symbols of perfection but of purpose.

The point of this digression into simple mathematics and geometry is to demonstrate that not only can the mind be related to structures based on the earth's rotation on itself and its revolution round the sun, but also to tangible natural phenomena as if indeed everything were, as Pico della Mirandola and Blaise Pascal claimed, mutually interconnected. Mathematics is a go-between uniting mind and matter in what we call experience. Structure helps to form, concretise and give meaning. Function is what we do with experience or what experience does to us. Perhaps it could be said that experience is structured function, whether actively pursued or passively endured.

An Ancient Symbol System

Amongst our structures we have discussed the role of astrology. Don't get fazed about astrology. It is not what you have been taught to believe or to disbelieve. Well-educated people tend to disbelieve. They have been told that it is bunk and they believe it. They have not tried to discover what it really is or to experiment with it and they have found no book explaining it in language to which they are accustomed. Look in any shop selling books on 'astrology' and one can readily see why. They would not be seen dead with such rubbish. So it is rejected a priori without examination and consigned to the tabloids and women's magazines. Less educated people have also not examined it but often tend to think there might be something in it; however, their interest rarely extends further than reading their favourite newspaper's 'astrologer'. So, with neither the academic, nor the scientist, nor the man in the street, nor the credulous knowing what they are talking about, the ignorance surrounding the subject is monumental. This is as much the fault of 'astrologers' as that of their denigrators, for few seem to have bothered to examine in depth the philosophical basis of the art they profess to practise.

This, of course, is a gift to critics, academics and scientists, for if by any chance astrology could be perceived to have more than a grain of truth, their world picture, indeed much of conventional thinking, would suffer a rude shock. So they have rallied to the cause of ignorance. They do not have to examine it as, in any other field of enquiry, they might in the name of science feel obliged to do. It is 'known' to be bunk, a priori. No need to go into it.

This situation caused me some disquiet. I am of an inquisitive nature. It occurred to me strange that a symbolico-mathematical system which had been taken up by every civilisation for considerably more than two millennia, more like three if one counts in the Egyptians and Chaldeans, should be written off in two hundred years as out-dated bunk by a now out-dated materialism. Though not myself an astrologer I began to look into the matter.

As I was brought up on classical Greek I started with Plato, since I knew Plato's *Timaeus* to be full of astrology. I also read Ptolemy's *Tetrabiblos* which is even more full of astrology. I then read Plotinus, who had written of astrology in one of his 'Enneads' while his biographer Porphyry, a neo-Platonist, having written a life of Pythagoras and an introduction to Aristotle's *Organon*, was an accomplished astrologer himself. I then read Nicholas of Cusa's well-known *De Docta Ignorantia* (*Of Learned Ignorance*). Nicholas was a cardinal, a mathematician and scientist who taught that the earth went round the sun a century before Copernicus came to the same conclusion. Reading Burckhardt's *Civilisation of the Renaissance in Italy* made me realise how much a part of life astrology played at that time. From there it was but a step to realise that not only Kepler but Galileo, Copernicus, Tycho Brahe and Newton had all studied astrology. Why? Newton also studied alchemy. What were they looking for? Obviously not fortune-telling. The most reasonable conclusion was that they recognised in astrology a symbol system related to the earth's rotation on its own axis and the revolutions of the planets which was meaningful and of heuristic value. As Wolfgang Pauli, writing on Kepler, recognised, the system supplied archetypes and 'image-formers' combined with mathematics and geometry which could serve as fruitful guides for developing thought in a bewildering world of radical change and exciting possibilities.

Eager to follow up this line of thought I read Kant's *Critique of Pure Reason* and Schopenhauer's *The World as Will and Representation* in which the latter had resuscitated in his own way Plato's 'phenomena' or 'appearances'. I then started applying modern philosophy to astrology. It was a revealing experience. I had not met anyone who had done so before or even heard of anyone. The ideas of some philosophers in this respect, Husserl for one, were very illuminating, as also were those of Hegel and Karl Popper. Hegel's interpretation of the 'dialectic' was very helpful, for dialectic plays an important part in astrology. Again Merleau-Ponty's *Phenomenology of Perception* suggested new insights into what the symbolism of astrology was capable of. I tackled Sartre's *Being and Nothingness* since Extentialism has relevance to the geometry of astrology, especially the horizon axis, which relates to immediacy, free-will and commitment. Finally I must not forget my personal favourite, Alfred North Whitehead, a Platonist and collaborator with Bertrand Russell in *Principia Mathematica*. All of these helped me put astrology into some sort of perspective. Moreover, since astrology has as a cardinal virtue a capacity for symbolic interrelation, it makes it easier to relate and compare one philosophy with another.

So much for philosophy. What of science? Materialism and reductionism appeared to have little relevance and their methodism was obviously inadequate to cope with the 'Gestalt' or holistic aspects of astrology. Relativity, and even more quantum theory, were, however, helpful. I owe much of my understanding of astrology to the physicists Werner Heisenberg, Erwin Schrödinger, Dirac and Pauli, none of whom were astrologers but whose ideas and discoveries gave me new insights into the mathematico-symbolic system I was examining. Heisenberg's *Physics and Philosophy*, Schrödinger's *What is Life?* and Richard Feynman's *QED* (Quantum electrodynamics) were especially helpful.

Reading back over the above I realise that I may have painted astrology in such glowing colours as to render it suspect rather than acceptable. It can, as in any other field bar mathematics, be all things to all men. Unlike science it does not seek accuracy or 'hard facts', and unlike science it does not have to retract or readjust its findings every few years, which is one of the troubles with hard facts. Astrology is concerned with ideas, with concepts, with symbols and movable patterns, with the mathematics of meaning. It does not get 'out of date' for it evolves with time and is geared to the revolution of time. What it does need is further investigation into its capabilities and potentialities, both philosophically and scientifically. I was pleased to see that the current *Oxford Companion to the Mind*, a work of some eight hundred pages, devotes two pages (some 1,600 words) to a critical but surprisingly not sceptical review of the subject.

Patterns of Genesis

Patterns in space relate primarily to sense-data and our world of appearances. Patterns in time relate more to mind. Both can be considered mathematically. Indeed, they have been for millennia. In Plato's Academy mathematics was *de rigueur*. Plato was much influenced by that quintessential mathematician Pythagoras, who believed that numbers lay at the root of everything. Plato did not go quite so far as that but nevertheless tried to fit things into a mathematical framework. Take the question of human gestation – the time taken from conception to birth. Plato thought that it conformed to a mathematical formula derived from the well-known theory of Pythagoras – the square on the hypotenuse is equal to the sum of the squares on the other two sides – the sides being those of a right-angled triangle in the ratio of three, four and five. This ratio is important, for as divisors of the 360° circle they result in the numbers 120, 90 and 72.

Plato's theory was that if children were to be born to develop to their best capabilities there must be an optimum time for conception and that this time was subject to a mathematical formula. He knew, of course, that the period of gestation roughly corresponded to nine solar, or ten lunar, months, something in the nature of 280 days, give or take a week or two, but this was not precise enough for his purpose. He also wanted to establish the earliest date at which a viable conception could occur. There was a symbolic background to his thinking. It was linked to the movements of the sun and moon as representing the male and female aspects of humankind. Nine months, being three-quarters of the year of 365.242 days (365.242 x 0.75), comes to 274 days (the solar contribution). The lunar contribution, in agreement with the equivocality of women, was two-fold. The moon has both a synodical and a sidereal revolution to be taken into account. The former is the period between two successive new moons. This month, the synodic month, is 29 days, 12 hours, 44 minutes, 2.7 seconds long. The sidereal month is 27 days, 7 hours, 43 minutes, 11.5 seconds long. The average of the above lunar revolutions is just over 28 days. The sidereal month is the moon's revolution measured against the fixed stars. The average of the moon's revolutions corresponds with the average human menstrual period. All the above figures are statistical averages. Neither nature nor individuals conform exactly to the rigidities of mathematics. Since the mean period of human gestation is approximately 280 days (nine solar months, ten lunar months: 28 x 10), the symbolic link with sun and moon is evident. Even the word period comes from the Greek *peri* meaning 'around' and *hodos* 'a way', in other words 'the way round' or revolution that both sun and moon regularly pursue.

The difference between the sun's period (274) and the moon's gestation period (280) is a mere six days. In Plato's day 6 was not just 6; it had associations. It was a perfect number $1 + 2 + 3 = 6$ and $1 \times 2 \times 3 = 6$. Six hours (6 x 60 minutes) is half the twelve-hour day. It is also one-sixtieth of the 360° circle, i.e, approximately one-sixtieth of the year. Six times the 12 months of the year comes to 72, which is $6^2 \times 2$. Seventy-two again relates to the average rate of heart-beat per minute of the average human being. It is perhaps not surprising, then, that primitive minds readily related mathematical periods to physical periodicity in human beings. In Plato's day it must have meant a lot more than it does to us today, though, of course, we also recognise circadian and other rhythms.

Now a child or an embryo is a solid figure and geometrically a solid figure is represented by a cube. Six cubed came to 216. Could it relate to the earliest period possible for the formation of a valid embryo? In Plato's *Timaeus* the ways in which numbers participate in the production of the human body is ingeniously if puzzlingly set out. The cube related to solidity, to body. In the fourth century AD Macrobius, writing on the soul and its destiny with relation to neo-Platonic doctrines and the astronomical and mathematical sciences, remarked that cubing makes a

solid body. With 280 days seen as the full period of gestation, 216 days seemed to fit in. The 64 days between the
first possible time and the best time, 64 days or seven
weeks, did not seem out of the way. Besides, as we have
remarked, nature itself continues to dodge the mathematical accuracies we attempt to impose on it.

What Plato apparently did, the process is not all that
clear, was to divide the 360° circle into twelve sectors representing the months of the year like an astrological
zodiac. 0° was the starting point and this was determined
by dividing a woman's life from the menarche (her first
menstruation) into periods of 216 days. The last menstrual period could then be seen as positioned at 0° in the
360° circle. Going round the circle clockwise, each 30°
sector designated a month, a favourable month being indicated by a favourable geometrical angle, 60°, 120° or whatever which the monthly sun made with 0° at the beginning
of the circle. This was, of course, a method derived from
astrology and quite in keeping with the claim that *The
Timaeus* was probably the first book on western astrology
ever written.

It is difficult nowadays to take such symbolic
numerology seriously. However, as symbolism, it is perhaps not so easily dismissable. There is indeed some evidence of a relationship between birth-times, conception-
times and angular relationships between sun and moon.
Some forty years ago a Czech medico, Dr. Eugen Jonas,
began checking on the birthdates and parturition dates of
patients in maternity wards. He began to notice that
births seemed to have some curious relationship with
solar and lunar revolutions. After further investigation he
came to the conclusion that the ability of a mature woman
to conceive tended to occur under exactly that phase of the
moon (sun–moon relationship) which prevailed at the
time she was born. There were other conclusions he came
to concerning determination of the sex of the child and its
viability, which further research failed to substantiate.
The time of conception, however, was another matter. Dr.
Jonas repeatedly achieved success rates of 80 per cent and
85 per cent. As was to be expected, his medical colleagues
were sceptical, though some were won over. The late Dr.

Rudolf Tomaschek, chairman of the International Geophysical Society, expressed interest, as also did Dr. Hilmar Haeckert, who dealt with the subject in his treatise *Lunationsrhythmen des menschlichen Organismus* (Leipzig, 1961). The Max Planck Institute of Heidelberg also sent for details and checked both data and calculations. However, as further investigations proceeded, corroborative percentages fell. The theory gradually ceased to arouse interest and apparently died.

There is, nevertheless, one factor which still seems to have some life in it, though not quite in the sense in which Dr. Jonas interpreted it. It concerns the relevance of sun-moon relationships not to the ideal time for conception but to the actual time, the moment when sperm penetrates ovum. Since this occurs not at the time of coition, but possibly some hours after, defining the precise moment is a problem and possibly unprovable. The theory, like that of Jonas, has astrological connotations. However, do not ask a newspaper astrologer about this. He will not know, if indeed he knows anything. Nor, indeed, as far as I can discover, will most professional astrologers know, since what is being set out here is not an accepted technique. But it works. Or rather, the combination of mathematics and symbolism can be seen to correspond with known fact.

Briefly the process is as follows. The researcher has to know the mother's horoscope and discover the number of degrees and minutes separating sun and moon at the time of her birth. This degree difference is operative for any of her children, for whom, if we know his or her date and time of birth, we can now set up a 'conception chart'. The researcher next sets up a birth chart for, say, her son. The position of the son's sun and moon is, for the moment, irrelevant. It is his mother's positions that are important. Since conception takes place roughly nine months before birth, if the son was, for example, born on the twelfth of August one has to consider his conception to have been probably somewhere within a week or two, or perhaps more, either side of the previous twelfth of November. The next move is to look back in an ephemeris or table of planetary movements to somewhere in mid-November of the year in question and discover a day in which his mother's soli-lunar relationship repeats itself exactly in degree distance. There will normally be two such dates within the month, one in excess of the normal period, the other short of it. If the birth is known to have been premature the later date is taken as relevant and vice versa. Whether the pregnancy was long or short, planetary positions on the relevant day will be seen to correspond by degree or geometrical angle not only with the son's natal chart but also with that of both his parents. The moment of sperm-ovum union symbolised by the soli-lunar relationship and determined by it could be significant on several counts. If true, it could perhaps determine questions of paternity, for the real father's chart should relate to the son's.

If true. Nothing is ever 100 per cent mathematically accurate, especially in biology. How can we check it? All the necessary data are available in the records of the British royal family, where all births, marriages and deaths have been meticulously recorded and made public for generations, though to my knowledge no such research has ever been done. Perhaps for obvious reasons. What scientist, for example, would want to verify what his training has taught him is nonsense?

What follows will show some of the links relating conception time to birth-time, to mothers' and fathers' birth-times, to those of grandparents and to corresponding links between each. The subjects are all members of the royal family. All corroborative links are within one degree of exactitude. For illustration we sketch out a 30° circle, each zodiacal sign containing 30°.

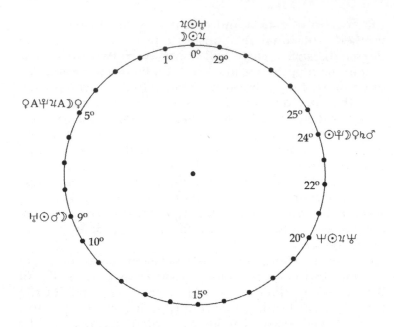

Princess Diana's soli-lunar angle was 225° 22', which gives us a date for William's conception – 17.9.1981. Going round the circle anti-clockwise from 0° to 29° 59' we insert planets and factors from the following members of the royal family: Prince William (conception chart and natal chart), Prince Charles, Princess Diana, the Queen and Prince Philip. Not all the available factors have been inserted, but those sharing a degree or geometrical angle with others are included. We first notice a cluster of factors around 0°. Prince Charles's Jupiter and Uranus are only minutes away, being in 29° 54' and 29° 55' respectively. Prince Charles's moon is in conjunction with the Queen's sun in Taurus, a difference of a few minutes only. Prince William's natal sun and Jupiter are also in the same degree. The close connection between two suns (mother and grandson) and the conjunction between sun and moon (mother and son) is noteworthy but not exceptional in families.

Moving on to the fifth degree, we find William's conception Venus and his natal moon, Prince Charles's

Ascendant (A), Diana's Jupiter and Pluto and Prince Philip's Ascendant and Venus. Around the ninth degree are William's conception moon and his natal Mars, also Diana's sun and Philip's Uranus. At the 22nd degree we find William's conception Neptune, Charles's sun and his mother's Jupiter and Neptune. Finally at 24° there is William's conception sun and his natal Pluto, Diana's moon and Venus together with the Queen's Saturn and Philip's Mars.

The above contacts are, of course, not all in the same zodiacal signs but, geometrically, those within each group are all in angular relationship with each other, i.e., conjunction, 30°, 60°, 90°, 120°, 150° or 180°, each of which indicates a meaningful symbolic link according to angle. One can trace such links even further back through generations or between related contemporaries. In our example it is worth noting that contacts are not evenly spaced around the circle but cluster about certain degrees. Such clusters tend to signal familial tendencies. After one has experimented in this line with different families the impression is gained that there are indeed patterns of development which can be mathematically and symbolically traced.

In my own family I have had plenty of opportunity for investigation. My grandfather had eleven children from two marriages, his second wife being younger than any of the children of his first wife. He was born in 1850 with sun in 3° Aquarius. My father was born in 1881 with sun in 3° Scorpio. I was born in 1911, my conception sun being in 3° Leo, the links forming one opposition (180°) and two quadratures (90°). I have birthdates for most of my extended family. The links are unmistakable. What does the conception chart signify? Unlike the birth chart it appears to have little symbolic relationship to a person's mental or physical potentialities. It is difficult to make sense of it when compared with one's knowledge of its owner. It does, however, often relate to a deep-seated mental or physical disorder not accounted for or hinted at in a normal horoscope. Or so it appears, for there has been little research in this field. If true it would appear to relate to hereditary rather than acquired disorder.

Plato and Jonas may have been wrong but, I suggest, in broad principle not far wrong. Moreover, the theory can be checked by anyone prepared to take the trouble. All that is needed is firm birth data and adherence to the not very difficult methodology and its accompanying symbolism.

Much of the information for this chapter comes from two sources:

1) *The Nuptial Number of Plato,* with a commentary by James Adam with an introduction by the architect Keith Critchlow. It was first published in 1891 but republished with Critchlow's contribution in 1985.

2) *The Lunar Cycle in Relation to Human Conception and the Sex of Offspring,* by F. Rubin, BA, BSc. (a short monograph of 15 pages published in 1967 but probably now out of print).

It's a Dog's World

We have been talking of our world as one of 'appearances' (phenomena), the sort of world that the prisoners in Plato's 'Cave' took for reality. Perhaps this needs a little further explanation. In Plato's *Theaetetus* the subject is introduced in a discussion of the well-known dictum of Protagoras, that 'man is the measure of all things'. On the face of it this seems undeniable. No measurement is possible without someone there to measure.

It is obvious that our world comes to us through our sense-organs. We see, hear, smell, touch and taste it. Without such organs it would not be there. It would nevertheless be there for those whose sense-organs were intact, but not for us. So our world is built up of sensation, or what scientists call sense-data, which come to us through our sense-organs, 'through' rather than 'by means of'. What we perceive through our senses is still not the whole world. Sensation has to be made sense of, and this involves our brain and mind. It is our mind which puts together the messages received through our sense organs and conjures up a picture of our world. Our world then 'appears' to us. And since each one of us is different we each conjure up a different world. You see the world in a different way from the way I see it.

Is there a world common to all of us as well as our private worlds? Obviously there must be or social life would be impossible. What comes through our sense organs is much the same for all of us. Since my sense organs are much the same as yours, our worlds appear much alike to see, to hear or to touch – we have a, more or less, common sense world on which we can all largely agree – an oak tree is an oak to both of us. Its when we begin to put things together in our minds, to make sense of sensation, that the trouble occurs. Minds are much more individual than senses. My mind is very different from yours. We

151

have been brought up differently, taught differently, had different parents, different schools and different experiences. So, unsurprisingly, we tend to think differently. A world which, to you, may appear delightful and full of opportunity, many appear to me a hell on earth. It is perhaps much the same world sense-wise but a totally different world in our minds.

Both our sense worlds and our mental worlds are appearances. It is we who conjure them up and bring them about. Without us they are not there. They can only be there in the way we experience them. And the opposite is true. We are creations of our world. Without our world we would not exist. We and our world hold each other up. Without the other each would collapse, for we are both part of each other, we part of it externally; it part of us internally.

There are many such worlds – as many worlds as there are living creatures to experience them. The world of a dog, for instance, may have trees and lamp-posts in it that we can recognise but in most other respects it would be totally alien to us. The smells would be enormously increased, colours decreased and its mental world almost non-existent. However, since we cannot ourselves get inside the dog to experience what he does we can only guess what his world might be like. He is unlikely, seeing the angle of the sun in the sky or perhaps looking in a puzzled way at something odd which happens to be a calendar, to conclude that this is May and a Thursday afternoon. The same goes, a fortiori, for the world of the lobster, the liver-fluke or the *bacillus coli*. Each creature tailors its own world to suit it and recognises no other. They are all appearances.

Such matters were the subject of discussion in Plato's *Theaetetus* nearly 2,500 years ago. In the eighteenth and nineteenth centuries, those ages of materialism following on The Enlightenment, such thinking was largely dismissed as outdated nonsense. Philosophically, however, such thinking never completely died and was resuscitated by Kant, Schopenhauer, Hegel and more recently by Bergson and Whitehead. If not at times scientifically acceptable it has always been a philosophically approachable matter. Now, with the body-blow to materialism delivered by relativity and quantum physics and the growing realisation in quantum theory that we and our world are one, we are already in a different ball game.

It is strange how science, almost against its will, has now, apparently, caught up with the ancient Greeks. What is stimulating is that the conventional, relatively closed and rigid parameters of materialism have now begun to open up. Frontiers are being crossed and new worlds discovered. Yet even here the Greeks had a prophetic word for it. The discovery of DNA and the immense ramifications of genetic science have two-thousand-year echoes. DNA is constituted of four acid bases – Adenine, Cytosine, Guanine and Thymine, shortened to ACGT. These are four basic letters of the genome code which lies at the root of every living thing, of life itself. They are part of a four-letter alphabet which repeats itself in different order – ACATGATATCCAATGT and so on ... and on ... and on.

This four-letter alphabet has a curious forerunner, as Professor Taylor in his critique of Plato's *Theaetetus* relates. In the *Theaetetus* Socrates dreamed that there were certain elements which were the ABC of nature. They formed syllables and complexes of letters and were not only basic to life but had meaning (*logoi*). Socrates's dream had a comparable analogy in the ideas of Empedocles a generation earlier. Empedocles's four 'elements', as Taylor notes, 'correspond exactly to the ABC of the book of Nature, bone, flesh and other tissues to "syllables", and organisms composed of these tissues to complete words'. Socrates and Empedocles were not alone. A similar idea was attributed to the Pythagorean, Ecphantus of Syracuse. Did those discoverers of DNA, Crick and Watson, read Plato, one wonders?

Exactness is a Chimera

The laws of physics are, one would suggest, approximate guides rather than rigid parameters. Nature is not exact; nothing living is perfect. There is always a little room for manoeuvre. Nature is alive and the fact that it is so depends on the loose, imprecise relationship between the real and the ideal. The circle of the year, 365.242 days, does not correspond precisely with the circle of geometry, 360 degrees. The planets do not describe perfect circles though their revolutions round the sun approximate, more or less, to circles, Venus the planet of beauty being the most circular. It is as though the particular strives toward the universal as the real to the ideal but never quite reaches its goal. Becoming strains toward Being but always falls short. Becoming is secular, Being eternal. Becoming is physically alive; Being is what Becoming aims at – perfection. In our phenomenal world exactitude is a chimera. Nothing in life is exact. Nature has room for both the rational and the irrational but it is the irrational that is natural. The rational may be something that nature strives for, that perhaps guides nature but never grips it in a rigid vice. It is, as it were, a lode-star, not a strait-jacket.

If nature abhors a vacuum, it no less discounts accuracy. Then what is accuracy for? It is surely a mark, a compass-point, an indicator of what to look for, but as a goal unattainable.

One of the most cherished laws of physics is the velocity of light. Nothing, it is claimed, can exceed the speed of light, though some scientists maintain that particles called tachyons can do so. But what is the speed of light? Scientists have tried to pin it down to a figure approximating 300,000 kilometres per second, but in fact it has apparently changed speed several times in recent years. Finally in 1972 and again in 1983, scientists, fed up with the persisting variations, decided to fix it by definition at the figure of 299.792458 kilometres per second with the claim that any future figure differing from this would be so small that it could safely be ignored. But according to Einstein's theory of relativity the velocity of light cannot vary; it is an absolute constant. The variations may, of course, be due to mistakes in measurement of the speed rather than in the speed itself. But then measurement, too, inevitably suffers from imprecision. Absolutely exact measurements do not exist, however many figures one counts after the decimal point.

Then again, what for instance is the velocity of light measured against? If everything is relative there is nothing *absolutely* stationary against which it can be measured. Its speed is measured relative to the observer and the observer himself is relative. Moreover, what enables the observer to measure the speed of light but the presence of light itself? Light can't be measured without light. We seem to be in a Catch 22 situation. To my unpractised mind the velocity of light is neither absolute nor constant. It is anthropocentric. Take away the anthropocentric relativity and light is at once instantaneous. It doesn't go anywhere at any speed. It is just here and there at the same instant. What makes it seem to take some eight minutes for the sun to come into our view is the subtle relative fact of ourselves. This is how it seems to us, and is to us, since that is the way we are and we cannot see it otherwise, for the world we live in is an anthropocentric world. In a perfect world light would have no speed. It would be instantaneous everywhere. One is reminded of Meister Eckhart's cryptic saying, 'The eye with which I see God is the same as that with which he sees me.' But Eckhart, being a mystic, had his eye not on our phenomenal world but on the perfect world of eternity and instantaneity.

The famous Einsteinian equation $E = mc^2$ (energy equals the mass multiplied by the speed of light squared) surely cannot be anything other than anthropocentric. Einstein was not dealing with the world of Being which, since it is perfect, is unreachable, but the imperfect world of Becoming, our world as we know it. As science has discovered, the equation works very well since both the equation and science and indeed ourselves are creations of our phenomenal world in which Eckhart's God is visible only to the eye of a mystic. Life as we know it would not be possible without imperfection or, indeed, without the passage of time, for time, too, is anthropocentric. As William Blake maintained, to 'hold Infinity in the palm of your hand and Eternity in an Hour' one must be in touch with another world more in tune with quality than quantity.

Colours, Metals and Numbers

We have touched elsewhere on the colour spectra of Goethe and Schopenhauer as opposed to that of Newton. The latter would appear to be more abstract. It relates to the numinous number seven, to the musical scale, to Mendeleef's table of elements, the seven days of the week, the creation of the world and the multitude of sevens which occur in The Book of Revelation. Seven appears to relate to matters that are half out of this world, other-worldly. Seven again is the only number in the first ten which has no whole-number answer when divided into the 360 degrees of the circle. With the spectrum of light and the celestial rainbow, with music and the Book of Revelation it could perhaps be seen as relating physics to the numinous.

Goethe's eight-fold schema seems closer to home. More, if you like, 'anthropocentric'. There is a curious structural rationality about it that is missing in Newton. Goethe, as we know, was acquainted with the symbolism of astrology. Colours in astrology and metals in alchemy are related to the sun, moon and planets. Metallic correlations are as follows: sun – gold, moon – silver, Mercury – mercury, Venus – copper, Mars – iron, Jupiter – tin and Saturn – lead. Colour associations are sun – orange, moon – indigo, Mercury – yellow, Venus – blue, Mars – red, Jupiter – purple, Saturn – green. We will illustrate the colour schema first: each planetary symbol opposes its opposite in meaning, sun – moon, Mars – Venus, Jupiter – Saturn, Mercury – Neptune.

In sequence the colours should be read clockwise from lowest to highest wavelength, from red round to violet. Goethe added purple to the seven, half-way between red and violet. Note that orange is half-way between red and yellow, green half-way between yellow and blue, indigo half-way between blue and violet. Psychologically colours have an effect on behaviour. Those to the left of the vertical are stimulating, those to the right relaxing.

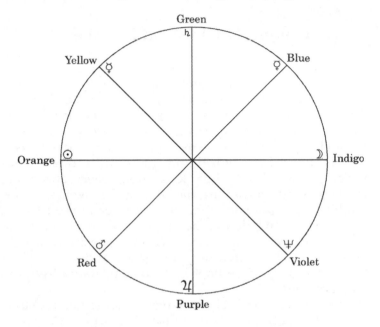

In alchemy and astrology planets are deemed to have an affinity with certain metals as well as with colours. The following circle, which has the planets in the same order as the previous one, each opposed by its opposite, can take us into a curious association with atomic number. The atomic number of an element relates to the number of electrons circling the atom of any particular element. The atomic number of gold is 79 since gold has room for 79 electrons circling the nucleus. Let us look again at our circle, this time with elements and atomic numbers instead of colours. Elements and their atomic numbers may be checked by reference to any chemistry textbook.

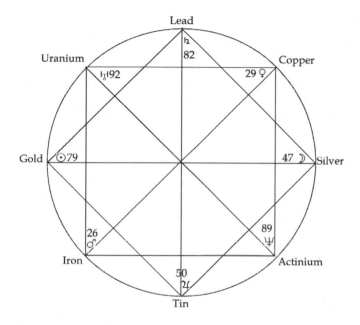

As compared with the previous circle, two changes in the ascription of elements have been made. Mercury is replaced by its 'higher octave' Uranus (Uranium) and Neptune by the element Actinium. The reason for the latter is that Neptunium is not a natural element, the last of the natural elements being Uranium. Neptunium, however, is in the 'Actinoid' series in Mendeleef's table of elements, so Actinium and its atomic number have been put in to replace it. In the accompanying diagram the relevant atomic numbers have been attached to each elemental symbol. Let us look first at the square formed by Gold – Tin – Silver – Lead and their respective atomic numbers. Gold plus Tin equals 129 while Silver plus Lead also equals 129; Lead minus Gold comes to 3 while Tin minus Silver also comes to 3. The difference between Silver and Gold is 32 while that between Lead and Tin is also 32. If we now take the diagonal Uranium – Actinium, the difference is 3 and the diagonal at right-angles to it, Iron – Copper, also differs by 3. The difference between Uranium and Copper is 63, as also that between Iron and Actinium. Finally Uranium 92 added to Iron 26 comes to

118 while Venus 29 added to Actinium also comes to 1i8.
We have an octagonal figure with two interlaced squares
and a multitude of atomic number relationships. Given
that several of such relationships must necessarily follow,
there seems to be a quite astonishing numerical coherence
here. Is this pure mumbo-jumbo or is there perhaps some
hidden principle behind it? To proceed further, Gold 79
plus Copper 29 amount to 108 while Lead 82 plus Iron 26
also come to 108. What is there that could connect these
two pairs? Well, if we look at tables of conductivity for
heat and electricity, for sound resonance, for shine or
lustre and for malleability, it comes out that gold and
copper can be forged whereas iron and lead can be cast,
the former pair being much more malleable. As for conductivity, gold and copper are more than three times more
conductive of heat and electricity than the other two.
Again, lead and iron have little resonance or lustre compared with gold and copper. In many ways the pairs are
antithetic, as are their planetary counterparts. Moreover,
108 is part of the 'quintile' series designated by 72 degrees,
one-fifth of the circle of 360, a relationship dear to Kepler.
The quintile series embraces the numbers 36, 72, 108 and
144, known respectively as semi-quintile, quintile, sesqui-
quintile and bi-quintile. The quintile is related through
the dodecahedron and the pentagram to that other pearl
of Kepler's, the Golden Section, and further to the logarithmic spiral and the Fibonacci Series on which we have
remarked elsewhere. Such numerical relationships may
seem far-fetched, and gold and copper, iron and lead
would appear to have little relevance here, but number
symbolism has sometimes proved surprisingly fruitful in
scientific discovery. One is tempted to say with
Baudelaire: 'Tout est nombre. Le nombre est tout. Le
nombre est dans l'individu. L'ivresse est un nombre.'

Structure is a noun, its description an adjective.
Function, however, is more of a verb, its description an
adverb. Their coming together engenders meaning.
Everything in nature, a palpable manifestation of those
universals' structure and function, has meaning.
Meaninglessness is meaningless. We have been talking of
atomic number, a code indicating the function of a struc-

ture, the atom. Different atoms have different structures, if only figurative ones, for the material existence of atoms is problematical even though, as hypotheses, we could not well do without them. Whether we regard them as real or figurative does not, for our purposes here, matter. The structure of each atom embraces a single, or several, figurative 'shells' within which its electrons are contained, jump out from or return to. Each element in the periodic table of elements has its characteristic number of electrons and shell structure within which the electrons 'orbit'. Even here in the differentiation of shells there is a curious numerical structure. The simplest atom, Hydrogen, has one electron and one shell within which it is considered to circle. With more complicated atoms, however, it turns out that the shells relate to a mathematical series of double squares. The first shell can accommodate 2 electrons (2×1^2) and is thus suitable for Helium as well as Hydrogen. More complicated elements demand both more electrons and more shells. The second shell may contain 8 electrons (2×2^2). The third shell can accommodate 18 electrons (2×3^2) and the fourth 32 electrons (2×4^2). With heavier elements the shells may be only sparsely filled and the double-square system fails to be all-compelling, leading to the instability of the elements concerned and suggesting the indeterminacy met with in quantum mechanics. Nevertheless the basic logical structure is arresting. Here we see structure applicable down to atomic level but below that, if it plays any part at all, giving way to the overpowering force of function and to uncertainty, with problematical particles apparently gambolling in unpredictable wave-functions.

More recently structure has made a bit of a come-back, in a field in which it would appear to have little relevance, 'chaos theory'. Its supporters include the mathematician Mitchell Feigenbaum, an enthusiast for Goethe both literally and scientifically, Benoit Mandelbrot, the discoverer of those beautiful ordered designs emerging from an orderless ground and named Mandelbrot 'fractals' after him, and Ilya Prigogine, the Nobel laureate, author of *Order out of Chaos*. Prigogine claims that order and structure can arise spontaneously out of disorder and chaos through 'self-organisation'. Structure, it seems, has something phoenix-like about it. New types of structure, which he names 'dissipative structures', can originate unbidden, of their own accord. Chaos, it seems, may be not only the death of order. It may also become its begetter.

Life Circles and Spirals

Patterns in space, in so far as they are regular, are fundamentally geometrical. In two dimensions we have the line, the plane, the triangle, the square, the pentagon, hexagon and so on. In three dimensions we have the tetrahedron, the cube, the octahedron, icosohedron and dodecahedron – the five perfect solids – together with imperfect solids and other imperfect plane figures. In the fourth dimension we have time. Time is conventionally graphically represented as an arrow pointing in a definite direction, in other words a straight line with a beginning and an end, and this is how we are conditioned to see life. It has a definite beginning and a certain end – birth and death. But this is a two-dimensional, spatial interpretation. Time cannot be so confined. Time, it is suggested, is circular or spiral. This idea, not by any means a new one, was known to the Greeks. The Pythagorean, Alcmaeon of Croton, said 'Man dies because he cannot join his end to his beginning.' But with a circle instead of a straight line he could do just that. He doesn't die. Parmenides, a little later than Alcmaeon, remarked 'It is all one to me where I begin for I shall come back there again.' Heraclitus, who preceded Parmenides by a few years, tells us that life and death are the same, 'the mortal is immortal, the immortal mortal'. Euripides wrote, 'Who knows if this experience we call dying is not really living, and if living is not really dying?' Aristotle was another who considered time to be circular. Plato, too, if the Myth of Er in *The Republic* is any guide and Socrates's remarks in *The Crito, Phaedo* and *Phaedrus*, also believed in the circularity and return of life.

Such circularity implies some kind of rebirth, with some a material rebirth or reincarnation, with others an immaterial one. After the Resurrection the early Christians also believed in reincarnation until, in the sixth century, for some reason I cannot recall, church authorities banned it and reincarnation became anathema. Christ himself appeared to believe in it. How else are we to interpret 'Before Abraham was, I am'? To come closer to our own time Friedrich Nietzsche believed in 'eternal recurrence'. That great champion of Darwin, the biologist T. H. Huxley, grandfather of Sir Julian and Aldous Huxley, believed in some form of reincarnation, as Aldous did himself. Even Sir Julian, biologist as he was, did not dismiss it out of hand.

The circular or helical representation of time could perhaps best be illustrated as a 'torus' or ring dough-nut. The torus we must imagine as a ring dough-nut around which is wound a spiral making several turns, the head of which eventually joins up with its tail to complete a circle, a corona of spirals. We have to imagine an hour torus, a day torus or a year torus according to the period of time we are considering. We can also envisage a life torus. In the hour torus 24 turns of the spiral complete the day. In the day torus 365 turns of the spiral complete the year. After a time events tend to repeat themselves, not exactly but reasonably recognisably. In the day torus the third morning may be like the first in that the sun rises, though one day it may be clear, the next obscured by clouds, the third by rain. In the year torus January one year may be much colder than January the next, or the next, but it is still January and still cold. January will never be July. The seasons play their part in this round ritual dance, coming round and round again, each time the same, each time slightly different, as suggested by the spiral. 'Last year was a good year for strawberries.' So, I suggest, it is with life. Everything changes and death is the name given to a life-change. After night there is a new day, with every spring a new year, with every death a new life. This is the cycle, the spiral of appearances among which are life and what we are taught to call death. The circle, however, is not to be confused with the spiral. The latter is endless, repeating and repeating, changing and re-changing. It represents potential in the process of actualisation, Becoming as opposed to Being. It is the Samsara of the Buddhists. On the other hand the circle is a perfect figure. Like the spiral it has no beginning and no end. It is out of time – eternal. It is Being to which Becoming strives. It is at the same time the structure that embodies and encompasses time. It is the womb of time – Plato's 'Receptacle'. Perhaps also it may represent Nirvana.

Structures and Functions of Colonialism

Governments are structures whose function is to control, organise, maintain and embody the aims and aspirations of a people. Sometimes the aims of government exceed or pervert not only the aims of its own countrymen but also of peoples over whom it has no rightful control. The concepts of empire and colonialism are instances. On 7 December 1975 the erstwhile Dutch colony, Indonesia, invaded the Portuguese colony East Timor. Over twenty years later the invaders are still there. The invasion massacred at least 200,000 East Timorese in which unspeakable atrocities were visited upon a largely defenceless people with the connivance of western nations and of Australia, East Timor's near neighbour. The military regime of the Indonesian dictator Suharto, which had already exceeded its function in subduing its own people, now sought to subdue others and was enabled to do so with the help or the indifference of Western nations, who supplied much of the invasion equipment including aircraft. The major Western contributor in arming the invasion force was Britain. Britain's policy apparently was that armaments could be supplied to countries for defence against their homeland but not for aggression against foreign nations or against their own people. Indonesia, however, did not fill the requirements on either of these counts. It was, nevertheless, continuing to be supplied with armaments by Britain whose government was turning a blind eye to its proclaimed policy. The population of Indonesia is one or the largest in the world, some 160 million; that of East Timor is minimal. Indonesia extends over thousands of miles. East Timor is about 150 miles by 50, a country barely the size of Wales. There was no way in which Indonesia could be said to be threatened by East Timor. Yet it was the aggressor Indonesia which Britain supplied with armaments, not the Timorese for their defence.

What prompted Britain to jettison even the ethical minimum respect tolerated by the armaments industry and
not only allow but actively assist the slaughter of thousands of innocent people? The answer can be found in
one word – profit. Not indeed profit for the people of
Britain as a whole, nor even for workers in the armament
industry, but for the directors, shareholders and the
Treasury – a handsome return.

Armaments are a highly profitable product and Britain
is in the forefront of their manufacture and sale. It is one
of the five largest suppliers of armaments in the world. If
it were not for the supply of armaments worldwide, wars
in Africa, Latin America, Asia and even Europe (Bosnia,
Kosovo) would be difficult or grind to a halt. Millions of
lives might be saved, cities spared from obliteration, vast
areas preserved from desolation, crops from destruction;
vegetation might not be poisoned, lands mined or children
maimed. How is it that all the massacres in Africa, in
Sierra Leone, the genocide in Rwanda and the starvation
of whole peoples such as in southern Sudan are possible?
They are possible largely because of armaments, only a
tiny proportion of which are of African manufacture. The
massacres and the genocide are kept going by our armaments, those of America, Britain, France, Russia and
China, countries that have each allowed themselves a
place at the top table – the nuclear powers – ostensibly to
keep the peace. Irony is not a strong enough word.

So why? Why do we not only persist in, but seek to
magnify, such lunacy? There would seem to be two main
answers, greed and aggression, both perversions of natural human propensities, the first a necessary acquisition
for the maintenance of life, the second a criminal misuse of
the drive and energy necessary for doing anything at all.
Individuals may endeavour to avoid this perversion of
natural drives but government and big business have no
such scruples, and against them the individual is powerless.

There are of course other factors. Crowd psychology
often plays a part, as Elias Canetti's *Crowds and Power*
graphically illustrates. Then again we have the domina-

tion–submission aspect, which we have recognised as occupying Cassirer's vertical axis, transferring its proper significance from the internal field of individual ethics to the outer field of social or political life, the recognition of justice, balance, parity and equivalence being replaced by superiority–inferiority, domination–submission. A people under attack from without will consolidate, co-operate, help each other, forget class distinctions and even sacrifice themselves for others while at the same time reserving a domination-submission posture *vis-à-vis* its external enemies. In war both emotion and reason are knocked off course and forced to act as lackeys to favour one's cause.

Snakes and Ladders

I have mentioned elsewhere that I suffer from, or rather I should say I enjoy a sort of 'serendipity', the ability to make unexpected connections or discoveries by chance. I am an untidy person and without serendipity I sometimes feel I would get nowhere. I repeatedly try to get some order into my bookshelves but rarely find, without a frustrating search, the volume I am looking for. Happily serendipity comes to my aid. The book I want falls to the floor, its pages often open at the passage I needed to refer to. Mental disorder and my bookcases seem to have some curious affinity hard to define. I am comforted by Paul Valéry's belief that disorder is a condition of a mind's fertility.

I was ruminating on the function of structure when serendipitously Jeremy Narby's book, *The Cosmic Serpent – DNA and the Origins of Knowledge*, came into my hand. The double helix of DNA would appear to be an epitome of structure imbued with a function involving not only the basis of evolution but of life itself. The structure was a ladder in the form of a double helix. But this was inescapably order and, if Valéry was right, surely lethal to fertility. However, he did in fact recognise the value of structure: 'Admirable parenté mathématique des hommes. Que dire de cette forêt de relations et de correspondances?' ('What can one say of this forest of relationships, this admirable mathematical human parentage?'). In DNA one cannot escape mathematics. It embraces the three–four mathematical arrangement we have noted elsewhere in fundamental structures. It contains just four bases or chemical compounds – Adenine, Guanine, Cytosine and Thymine – which have simple molecular structures, but which nevertheless are mind-provoking. Two have a six-atom structure (Cytosine and Thymine). The other two have a nine-atom structure. The first two form hexagons, the last two form combined hexagons and pentagons. The six of the hexagons and the nine of the hexagons/pentagons are of course multiples of three. If we take the four bases multiplied three times we get 4 x 4 x 4 = 64, reminiscent of the 64 answers to the riddle of life in that curious structure of the Chinese, the *I Ching* or *Book of Changes*. If the *I Ching* represents the hidden, mental intercommunication between the individual and the universal mind, DNA does much the same in the physical, biological world. Whatever view one takes of the *Book of Changes,* not only Leibniz but also a number of Nobel laureates valued it, as also did Carl Jung.

With DNA we appear to be on the frontier between the rational and the intuitive, for the double helix has a further double in the minds of primitive Amazonian shamans. Under the influence of a medicinal and hallucinatory plant, 'ayahuasca', they were able to conjure up a fascinating display of 'snakes and ladders', the snakes being representations of Jeremy Narby's 'Cosmic Serpent' while the ladders were strongly reminiscent of the double helix. Narby, an anthropologist who lived among Ashaninca Indians in the Peruvian part of the Amazon basin for a period of two years, was amazed by the knowledge of the properties of hundreds of plants gained by tribal shamans. It was far ahead of what western botanists and chemists had managed to discover, yet they had none of the scientific expertise and technology which the latter enjoyed. How had they been able to achieve what western science had not? The answer was the rigorous disciplines entered into by shamans in pursuit of their prophetic 'hallucinatory' visions. In addition to the drinking of ayahuasca, they abstained from sexual relations, avoided fats, alcohol, salt, sugar and condiments. They ate bananas and fish which, though they did not know it, were rich in serotonin, a brain hormone and neuro-transmitter. Their methods, to western minds, might have appeared highly questionable but their results were not, for the plant properties discovered by such means were later confirmed in laboratories. Many of the ayahuascan-promoted visions appeared to conform loosely with the ancient and now ridiculed 'doctrine of signatures', in which the shape and colour of a plant gave a clue to its possible medicinal use. A yellow plant, for instance, might be useful in cases of jaundice. But ayahuasca appeared to provide the shamans with much more precise information than that.

By far the most startling of shamanic discoveries, however, was the structure of DNA's double helix which the western world discovered in the 1960s at Cambridge through the efforts of Crick and Watson. Narby, however, asserts that the shamans of the Amazon region of Peru have known of the double helix structure for centuries. They did not of course recognise it as the structure of DNA but they did see in it the life-force of which DNA is the prime paradigm. Pictorially the visions of the shamans and the reproductions of the double helix in our biology textbooks are essentially the same.

Snakes and ladders. Both went up and down, fuelled by fasting and ayahuasca, and they were often highly coloured. Narby himself, under the influence, confirmed their presence. Both snakes and ladders had counterparts in conventional science. The snakes are visible microscopically as two sister chromatids of each chromosome in the early prophase stage of development of the process of life. They correspond with the visionary snakes seen by the shamans. The ladders of the double helix, the rungs of which are formed of the four bases, Adenine, Guanine, Cytosine and Thymine, correspond with the ladders seen by the shamans, the sides of the ladders being two long snakes twisting in the same way as the double helix twists. Narby suggests that the DNA structure is rooted deep in man's unconscious as well as physically in his body. He claims it has been known to primitives and has been part of the hidden knowledge of the ancient world for centuries. He instances the caduceus of both Hermes and Aesculapius. This potent myth is, moreover, not confined to the Amazon basin. It has been a vision of shamans worldwide, even as far away as Australia. Although Narby does not mention it, the serpent and the ladder are represented in astrology. There Hermes is construed as his Roman equivalent Mercury, whose associated zodiacal sign is Gemini, The Twins. In astrology Mercury represents intelligence and its sign Gemini the intellectual and physical dialectic only possible with a duality. It corresponds with the twin snakes and the double helix. More specifically the snake or serpent is symbolised by the sign Scorpio but this sign also symbolises the dragon (tauros drakontos pater, as the Greeks had it) – the bull, taurus, the opposite sign, is the father of the dragon, another instance of duality and dialectic. Yet again, and on a higher level, Scorpio symbolises both the eagle and the phoenix. It is the sign of death and rebirth. The scorpion and dragon stand for death, the phoenix rising from the ashes stands for rebirth, the serpent and the eagle relate to both life and death. The sign Scorpio is also the sign of sex as well as of death – Eros and Thanatos – and, as many have remarked, sex is itself a kind of death, as indeed it is of life. At a deeply psychological level Scorpio can be profoundly, and sometimes explosively, revelatory – almost 'shamanistic'. Astrologically speaking the rational, scientific aspect of DNA relates to Gemini and Mercury, the subconscious shamanic visions to Scorpio and its associated planet Pluto. Scorpio also has associations with venom, poison and drugs, Pluto with discoveries in depth.

The snake or serpent has always been connected not only with poison or venom but also with medicine; hence its adoption as an emblem by the medical profession, the serpent usually curled round a pole or pillar. It has also been associated with knowledge, wisdom and the life process. We have the story of the serpent in the Garden of Eden as the symbol of the knowledge of good and evil. We have the serpent that swallows its own tail, the 'ouroboros', and the serpent that encircles the universe as in Indian mythology, or again the Indian 'Kundalini' or serpent power which lies curled like a serpent at the base of the spine (a part of the body symbolised by the sign Scorpio) but which can be awakened and shoot up the spine through the 'chakras' to the crown of the head. In ancient myths in many countries serpents abound. Myth is a word much misunderstood, often nowadays used pejoratively as something which is false or unprovable or ridiculous. However, myth, as people like Malinowski and Mircea Eliade have pointed out, is a concept rich in associations and meaning. Myths are subtle conceptual structures giving form, however vague or cryptic, to what is beyond the reach of reason. Shamans are both creators and interpreters of myths.

My second encounter with serendipity occurred within a day or two of my first. It arrived in the guise of the current edition of *New Scientist* in two parts. The first was a reported interview with the neuropsychologist Brian Butterworth concerning his new book *The Mathematical Brain*. Butterworth claims that there is a 'number module' in the brain and that it is both innate and instinctual. Basic counting, he says, comes naturally. 'Even remote tribes can count even if they have no words for numbers.' Have we not come upon something like this before, for instance Chomsky's syntactic structures and the linguistic claims of the French structuralists? And can we not go back yet much further to Plato's *Meno*? In the *Meno* Socrates's main standpoint is that one does not have to stuff information into the brain; one has to pull it out. It is already there, basically. What one has to do is to act as midwife and bring it to birth. Socrates demonstrates an experiment to prove this. The subject of the exercise is a slave-boy who, as he thinks, knows no mathematics. Socrates proves that though the boy is not aware of it, the mathematics is there in his head already and only has to be brought out by questioning, not by teaching. Neither Plato nor Socrates of course knew anything of Butterworth's 'number module'. But they all, Butterworth, Chomsky and the structuralists, whether they had read Plato or not, seemed to assume some innate pattern of information to which the mind had access, module or not. The moral is not to stuff the mind with facts. Intelligence is demonstrated by the ability to bring to birth what is already there.

The second part of my serendipitous dip into *New Scientist* concerned the functions of the two halves of the brain. To go back for a moment to Narby; his book includes two shamanic illustrations of the human brain. They are crude and simple. The longitudinal fissure in the roof of the brain which divides the two hemispheres is in the one case occupied by an anaconda, in the other by twin snakes, an anaconda and a rainbow boa. They are copied from Reichel-Dolmatoff's *Brain and Mind in Desana Shamanism*. The Desana, a tribe of which the shamans are ayahuasca drinkers, apparently believe that the longitudinal fissure was formed 'in the beginning of time' by the cosmic serpent, the anaconda. In the second illustration the two snakes entwined symbolise a male and female principle.

Now we come to the second piece in *New Scientist*. It was written by John McCrone and entitled 'Left Brain, Right Brain'. I was interested to discover whether the left and right hemispheres might be related to a 'male and female principle' as suggested by the Desana snakes. Not, I gathered, in so many words. But there were very interesting differences which one might attribute broadly to one sex or the other. Brain hemispheres and their function have been a popular subject of discussion in recent years and much of what has been asserted does not, according to the writer of the article, bear examination. However, further research has come up with some interesting results and, in one case, a complete reversal of what had been claimed. A brain-scanner test appeared to demonstrate that the left brain focused on detail, on close-up, and on particulars, while the right brain registered, rather than focused on, a broad, panoramic or general background in which, instead of objects being split apart spatially they were here interconnected and interrelated. The left saw the grammar and syntax; the right saw the meaning of the sentence, paragraph or book. Though the writer does not say so, there seems to be a perceptible framework to each hemisphere within which a plethora of related concepts might be contained. It is perhaps not too absurd for the reader to connect by analogy the left brain with split-second time, digital watches, particle physics, reductionism, microscopical research and precision as against the right brain's duration in time, analogue watches, wave physics, holism, macroscopic or telescopic research and approximation rather than precision. Extrapolating further we could perhaps say that reason and logic should find a place in the left brain, imagination and intuition in the right.

There is, however, a difficulty. An account of the

research was published in *Nature* in August 1996. Further research, however, though confirming hemisphere differences, turned the whole concept upside-down and the unfortunate research team had to publish a paper saying the precise opposite. The right brain had taken over the left brain's property and vice versa. The two Desana serpents seem rather prone to swapping sides. The serpents, however, do not separate. They still remain mutually entwined. It would appear that though the two brain hemispheres are separated by the longitudinal fissure there is still quite a bit of traffic both ways across the commisure, the corpus callosum. The hemispheres, too, are metaphorically if not physically intertwined. Neither side is wholly 'male' or 'female'. The brain is a hermaphrodite. If there are two sides the one complements rather than contradicts the other.

But how does one explain the change of sides? Could we get, perhaps, a helping hand from philosophy? The pre-Socratic Heraclitus, the Taoist Chuang-Tzu, the philosopher Hegel and the psychologist Carl Jung all claimed that, as Chuang-Tzu said, 'That which is one and that which is not-one, is also one'. Heraclitus said much the same in his 'Harmony in contrariety' and was the first to teach the 'dialectic'. Hegel developed the dialectic, and Jung, influenced by Heraclitus, taught the 'coniunctio oppositorum', the coming together of opposites through 'enantiodromia' (Gk, enantios – opposite, and dromia – a running). In Hegel's dialectic the opposites united in synthesis – the two united within the one and indeed became one. Perhaps the change of sides in the attributions of the two brain hemispheres is an instance of 'enantiodromia' resulting in 'harmony in contrariety'.

From Pyramid to Precession

For certain structures of physically hard, earthy composition it has been difficult to discover an adequate or relevant function. Take, for instance, the pyramids of the Maya civilisation in Mexico or the pyramids of Egypt. Recent research has suggested that they both originated much earlier than conventional opinion was prepared to admit. Then what was their function? What were they for? One does not build a massive carefully aligned structure such as a pyramid for nothing. Until comparatively recently such structures were loosely associated with ideas of religion, of burial or of life after death. However, the mathematical precision of the construction and the exactitude of their positioning, especially in the pyramids of Egypt, suggest a scientific rather than a religious intention. Why should religion require the exactitude of minute fractions of the perimeter of a circle? The Great Pyramid of Cheops at Giza, the largest, heaviest and probably the oldest stone building on the face of the earth, was constructed to minute tolerances and oriented with astonishing accuracy to accord with the north and south poles. The builders even employed the ratio 'pi' (π) – the ratio of the circumference of a circle to its diameter, i.e., 3.14 ... – in their construction of the pyramid. This ratio has been, and often still is, attributed to the Greek Archimedes in the third century BC, yet the builders of the Great Pyramid had used it over two thousand years earlier. The minute accuracy achieved by the architects of the pyramids of Giza rivals even that of present-day technology. This surely suggests a scientific rather than a historico-religious function.

A similar objection applies to the use of the Golden Section (ϕ) 'phi', a ratio of 1.618 ... whose discovery is attributed to the Pythagoreans of the sixth century BC. Yet here again the ratio 'phi', the Golden Section, has been

176

found in the construction of the King's Chamber in the Great Pyramid of Cheops, antedating Pythagoras again by at least two thousand years. The suggestion of a scientific intent is further strengthened. There is no proof, of course, that 'pi' remained unknown until the time of Archimedes or that 'phi' only came to light with the Pythagorean Greeks. But there is proof of the contrary, and the proofs are enshrined in the architecture of the Great Pyramid.

The pyramids of Giza are situated and oriented on the surface of the earth with such precision that there would appear little room for accident. The longitude and latitude of Giza is 30° North and 31° East, a map reference which turns out to be the focal point of the entire land-mass of the whole planet. Moreover, it lies at exactly the third of the distance from the equator to the north pole. Latitudinally it stands on the thirty-first meridian, i.e., one-sixth of the distance between 0° and 180° (the Greenwich Meridian and the International Date Line), i.e., one-twelfth of the whole circumference of the earth at that latitude. A terrestrial focal point if ever there was one.

Terrestrially accurate the pyramid may be, but its construction appears to suggest an even greater celestial significance. Built into the Great Pyramid are angles exactly matching the obliquity of the ecliptic (the sun's path as seen from the earth). The obliquity is the angle between the plane of the earth's orbit and that of the earth's equator (now about 23° 27', though it varies from 22° to 24.5°). This tilt of the earth's axis of rotation gives us our changing seasons. The tilted earth also wobbles like a top clockwise, producing a phenomenon called 'the precession of the equinoxes' (equal night – equal day corresponding to 21 March and 21 September) which themselves *precess* gradually clockwise round the ecliptic (the zodiac). The precession is exceedingly slow, taking nearly 26,000 years to complete the circle. What, however, is the point, the function of embodying the mathematics of the obliquity of the ecliptic and the precession of the equinoxes in the construction of the Great Pyramid?

Some researchers have suggested the prediction of global changes in climate and temperature such as the

Great Ice Age.   Professors Hays and Imbrie of the US
National Science Foundation have calculated in their
paper 'Variations in the Earth's Orbit. Pacemaker of the
Ice Ages' (*Science*, 10.12.1976) that the onset of ice ages can
be predicted when such celestial cycles display maximum
eccentricity and minimum obliquity combined with the
precession of the equinoxes. All such data are apparently
obtainable in the precise mathematical construction of the
Great Pyramid, suggesting that the pyramid itself was
much older than convention believes and was built in the
humid climatic period resulting from the melting of the
last ice age.

I have in my possession a copy of Giorgio de Santillana's
The Origins of Scientific Thought. De Santillana, Professor
of the History and Philosophy of Science at the
Massachusetts Institute of Technology, is no starry-eyed
crank but in 1969 he teamed up with a German professor,
Hertha von Dechend (Professor of the History of Science
at Frankfurt University). Between them they wrote
Hamlet's Mill, a thesis on ancient myth connecting universal myths with global cataclysms. They claimed to
have discovered the traces of a scientific language coded
in myth thousands of years older than the civilisations of
Egypt and Sumer. In the mathematics of the Great
Pyramid, constructed, according to its own measurements,
in the period following the Great Ice Age, could we not
have a vivid example of such a language?

We have discussed structures in the mind, geometrical
structures, structures in nature and man-made structures.
In the language of Plato's *Timaeus* structure occupies the
lowest rung in his ladder of 'elements', that of the element
Earth. Structure's complement in this particular 'continuum', function, rises on the other hand up through the
elements, transmuting structure as reciprocally the latter
relaxes control over function. The one's loss is the other's
gain. The one's inertia the other's dynamism. As the one
waxes the other wanes. If we now look at Cassirer's two
axes, the meridian–horizon cross, it will be seen that logically structure must occupy the horizon, function the
meridian axis, since structure is predominantly static and
extended in space, function predominantly dynamic and

extended in time; the former relates to matter, the latter to energy, and energy, as Einstein has proved, equals mass multiplied by the square of the velocity of light.

Does this holy trinity, energy – mass – light, hold further secrets for us than science will so far admit? Can it be related metaphorically to function – structure – enlightenment? In our phenomenal world 'everything flows', as Heraclitus reminded us 2,500 years ago. Even the most solid structure is not completely static. Even the pyramids change with time, however slowly. The diameters of Ernst Cassirer's meridian–horizon cross are not perennially anchored on the same spot. They rotate with time. Structure gives way to function – function to structure. They rotate at various speeds, one of which is related to the 24-hour day (a circadian rhythm), another to the 12-month year (an annual rhythm), one rhythm obedient to the rotation of the earth on itself, the other to its revolution round the ecliptic. There are also other periodic revolutions.

In the rotation of the earth on itself the two poles of the horizontal relate to equality of light and dark, sunrise and sunset, while the two poles of the meridian relate to extremes of light and dark, midday and midnight. In the revolution of the earth round the sun the two poles of the horizon relate to the mean ratio between light and dark in the rhythm of the year, the spring and autumn equinoxes (the First Point of Aries and of Libra) about 21 of March and September. At this time the hours of light and dark are equal, and equality is one of the attributes of the horizon. The two poles of the meridian or the vertical, however, relate here not as above to midday and midnight but to midsummer and midwinter, the summer and winter solstices, the extremes of light and dark, the longest day and the longest night. In both the revolution of the earth and its rotation round itself we see structure, function and light brought together in a meaningful cyclical dance.

Structure and function embrace categories of kindred concepts, and cross-fertilisation between them can sometimes throw up unexpected and fruitful results. Even when several levels of significance are involved they will

often be seen to involve 'families' of meaning. In
Wittgenstein's *Philosophical Investigations* he describes relationships between categories of meaning and represents
them as 'forming a family'. It is not difficult to relate any
particular meaning to its appropriate family of kindred
meanings, as a thesaurus graphically illustrates, though
just what it is that makes one meaning a member of a certain family may be difficult to define. Nevertheless one
can recognise the family resemblance.

The same general meaning can be seen to occupy different poles at different times. While seen at one level,
structure considered as a framework for social interaction
between people should naturally occupy the horizontal
axis, but when seen as an ethical code, or even a structure
of government, it should logically occupy the upper pole
of the vertical axis. There are innumerable logical
relationships which can be discovered within or without
families of meaning if this is borne in mind.

I am not being dogmatic about this. There are no doubt
inconsequences of logic and errors of fact in the above.
The reader should not take me at my word. It is not facts I
am after. It is ideas. I distrust exactitude. It is a fiction
and never achievable in this world. To my mind it is
approximation which is important. It provides interstices,
fissures in the rock wall of existence in which, like the
saxifrage, nature and life can root. Even if our structure is
faulty the cracks in it may yet harbour fruitful soil.

Our Debt to the Classics

The value of structure in philosophy and in scientific discovery was recognised some two and a half thousand years ago. Many of the problems of modern science were first raised among the ancient Greeks. An atomic theory was the child of Leucippus and Democritus. Plato was responsible for recognising our phenomenal world as one of appearances, and his description of the elements and 'regular solids' was a forerunner of modern stereo-chemistry. He also fathered the ideas of 'universals' and teleology. Internal teleology (entelechy), evolution and the idea of potentiality (Lat. 'potentia', Gk. 'dynamis') and classification (taxonomy) we owe to Aristotle. The reconciliation of opposites (enantiodromia) was taught by Heraclitus. In the sixth century BC Pythagoras experimented with mathematics and geometry and made the first rational discovery of pitch and harmony in music. Pythagoras, it would appear, was an even greater polymath than Leonardo da Vinci. Bertrand Russell said of him: 'I do not know of any other man who has been as influential as he was in the sphere of thought.'

In his book *Physics and Philosophy* the Nobel physicist Werner Heisenberg gives practically a whole chapter to the value of Greek original ideas. It is not generally known, and Heisenberg doesn't refer to it, that his father was a Greek scholar and Heisenberg himself could read Plato's *Timaeus* in the original Greek. He claimed also that if one wanted to make radical discoveries one had better go back not to the latest advances in science but to the very origins of scientific thought, and in his case that meant the ancient Greeks. The Greeks set up the structures upon, or within, which philosophy and science developed and when we are in the business of scientific discovery we still go back to them as, in effect, Einstein did.

A. N. Whitehead, Russell's erstwhile tutor at Cambridge, has remarked that Newton would have been nonplussed by quantum theory whereas Plato would have welcomed, if not expected, it. The thought structures set up by the ancients are often still valid for modern use. It need not be the Greeks. It might equally be the Indians or the Chinese, as many scientists such as Schrödinger, Bohm, Capra and others have discovered.

Damn the Dam

Western nations, including our own, have been tempted to support the construction of the Ilissu Dam in eastern Turkey. This, since it will affect both the rivers Euphrates and Tigris, to say nothing of Iraq and Syria, will have international complications. Turkey does not want to listen to the protestations of these two countries. To the Turkish Government, since both rivers have their source in Turkey, the dam is theirs to do with as they want regardless of the threat to those countries through which the rivers flow. Furthermore the people chiefly affected by the dam and whose lands are being flooded and their lives and futures put at risk are the Kurds, a people long terrorised by both Turks and Iraquis. At the moment it looks as if Western profit and Turkish nationalism are unstoppable. A whole people is in danger of being sacrificed to the greed and pride of those in control.

In his book *The Physicist's Conception of Nature* Werner Heisenberg tells a pertinent story, for it concerns irrigation. A Chinese peasant was working on his vegetable plot. He went down a well with a bucket, filled it with water, brought it up and poured it into his ditch. A passer-by, watching him, thought this was hard effort to little effect. He spoke to the peasant and asked him whether he wouldn't like to know of a more effective way of doing the job. The peasant replied: 'And what would that be?' The passer-by said: 'You simply take a wooden lever weighted at the back but not at the front and attach a bucket to it. You can then raise the water so quickly and easily that it gushes out. It's what is called a "draw-well".' The peasant was not impressed. 'Whoever uses machines', he said, 'does his work like a machine. He carries the heart of the machine in his breast. He loses his simplicity and the strivings of his soul. He himself becomes a machine. I know about such things as your lever but I am ashamed to use them.'

Substitute the Kurds for the Chinese peasant. Their land, which has been flooded against their will, was their vegetable plot. The buckets they used have been replaced by an immense dam, one of the largest in the world. For whose benefit? Not theirs. They have lost everything. They have had to move their villages to barren land higher up and have lost not only their homes but their livelihoods also. For whose benefit then? Not for the peasants of Iraq or Syria either, who may eventually be conscripted in a war against Turkey to defend their own access to the water they need. The benefactors, as usual, are those whose need for water is much less critical, Western construction firms and the Turkish Government, where the flow of water is rapidly converted into a flow of dollars. The process of turning the soul into machinery or the life of a whole people into a source of profit for their rulers is well oiled and smoothly efficient. We do not, of course, believe in souls anymore, only in genes. We have wallets instead, and of course technology. Yet, out of date as it may seem, perhaps the Chinese peasant had a point.

The dam was a material structure whose function was the provision of water for the benefit of Turkey, that for Kurdish peasants secondarily and that for Iraquis and Syrians not at all. The structure directed the function in favour of those who dreamed up the structure. To others the dream was a nightmare. But they were not asked. Structures are always two-faced. They prop up, protect and support on the one hand; alienate, eliminate and imprison on the other. Which face should support whom and which should imprison whom is decided by the constructors and paymasters and inevitably it is constructed to favour them, while the function tends necessarily to follow the structure. The size of the structure is also important – a bucket does little harm; a vast dam can submerge the lives of thousands and possibly trigger a war.

Euripides and The Battle of Salamis

We have discussed the role of 'potentia', like mathematics, as an intermediary between ideal and real. Potentia presents us with a sort of 'limbo', lurking without visible support but capable of 'potentially' materialising concepts into actualisation, of converting a latent fluid activity into an actual tangible structure – turning a fiction, if you like, into a fact. Such a transformation, it seems to me, is accompanied by a symbolic coincidence and coherence. The potentiality is not precise but embraces a broad characterisation factor; in its progression towards actuality the imprecise progresses toward greater precision. The vague potentiality branches out into a multiplicity of possible events originating from a common source. Some of these possibilities become actualised in particular occurrences. Others may never materialise and remain 'in potentia'. What is the actualising factor? It is surely, as in quantum physics, the event itself and our observation of it. The character of the event is an amalgam of the actuality and our appreciation of it. The concentration or pin-pointing of the event, should it eventuate, is brought about by the coming together of three factors. We have a triangle of co-ordinates – space/time/event.

Suppose we take as an event the Battle of Salamis, which took place at Salamis on a certain day in September, 480 BC. Other events must necessarily have taken place on that day but not on the precise spot of the battle. Similarly, other events must have taken place at Salamis but not at that time. Different events cannot very well occupy the same space at the same time. Only the battle united both time and place in the event itself. The main characterisation of the event would appear to be that of violence or war, whether experienced physically or mentally. Another event which occurred at approximately the same place and time was the birth of Euripides, since he

185

first saw the light of day on the island of Salamis while the battle was raging. Could there be any connection, actual of symbolic, between the birth of Euripides and the Battle of Salamis? We have suggested that a characterisation of the latter event might well be that of war. Well, as it happens, Euripides was noted for his attitude to war. He was disgusted with it, as can be inferred from his plays *The Trojan Women*, *Andromache* and *Iphigenia in Aulis*.

C. G. Jung often noticed the coincidence of events of symbolic similarity and evolved a concept of 'synchronicity'. An Austrian scientist by the name of Kammerer had come to a rather similar conclusion and embodied it in his 'Das Gesetz der Serie' (The Serial Law). Kammerer was ridiculed at the time but Einstein was persuaded that there might be something in it. Jung claimed that events occurring at the same time and place appeared to partake of a broad similarity of characterisation. He instanced that a wine was characterised by its timing, its vintage and also by the soil and climate in which the vine grew. To him it appeared that each space/time/event had its own character which, if broad in potential, could be surprisingly precise in actual reality. For instance a vintage wine unlabelled could often be dated and its provenance named by an expert sommelier.

We have perhaps stretched the elastic of belief rather more than usual. It would be much easier and safer to stick within the firm walls of orthodox opinion where tautology succeeds tautology in a self-congratulatory embrace. But safety is not a recipe for theoretical discovery, however necessary it may be for physical conservation. A little risk-taking is sometimes not only advisable but even indispensable. Salamis was a risk which paid off for the Greeks. Euripides took risks in his writing and became as a result extremely unpopular. His defence of women, his irony, his social criticism and his disillusionment with accepted standards made him many enemies. War, which he despised, he brought upon himself in the theatre. Was the Zeitgeist, or rather Zeit/Raum -geist, at fault? Did the seed of his vine bearing fruit in the soil of Salamis stamp a certain cachet on the wine it produced and the blood it symbolised? Perhaps a little. The jury is still out. There is always more to be learnt, for tomorrow may well contradict today.

The Battle of Salamis was the mental arena for the coming together of the thoughts of Aristotle and those of the Polish logician Jan Lukasiewicz. The latter was a follower of Aristotle but nevertheless came to the conclusion that Aristotle's claim that opposites mutually destroyed each other was not complete. A third term was necessary, which he designated as 'neuter'. He instanced the event of the Battle of Salamis. Suppose somebody beforehand said that the battle would take place. At the time this was said it was certainly not false, though it had not yet occurred. But if it was true, the battle would seem to have been predetermined. It was therefore neither true nor false. It was neuter, and its truth or falsity could only be confirmed by the event, the battle itself, or by its failure to materialise.

Surely something similar can be recognised in a totally different field, that of quantum physics, in which an event may be 'in limbo' (cf. the famous example of 'Schroedinger's Cat') and is actuated one way or another by the participation of an observer. Indeed, did not Aristotle himself provide for something similar in his concept of 'potentia'? How, one may ask, can it come about that the Battle of Salamis may act as a focal point for threads connecting Euripides, Aristotle, Jung, Kammerer, Lukasiewicz and quantum physics? I am aware, of course, that to a logician or to a scientist this is, perhaps, stretching the elastic of permissible thought to breaking point and beyond. But I believe in stretching points, crossing frontiers and fracturing structures. I regard them as guides, not barriers. One never knows what may lie beyond. Perhaps Pico della Mirandola and Bell's theorem in quantum physics had a point – everything is connected to everything else.

The Sensitive Plant

We have not given much space to function as a necessary concomitant of structure. Each is in need of the other's presence. Plants appear to lack the nervous structure of animals and were therefore considered not to be able to feel or to respond to stimuli, while animals, provided with such a structure, could. Indeed, when Prince Charles was noticed talking to plants the reaction, not only of the tabloid press but also of the man in the street, was 'He must be off his head. Plants can't feel.' None of his critics seems ever to have heard of Sir Jagadish Chandra Bose. Bose was a Bengali scientist who had the good fortune to have been a pupil of Lord Rayleigh, a Nobel prize physicist who discovered argon, and of Francis Darwin, Charles Darwin's son. Bose was a physicist as well as a biologist and botanist. In 1895, imbued with the spirit of Clerk Maxwell in the electromagnetic field, he transmitted electric waves from one room through three intervening walls to another room seventy-five feet away. This was a year before Marconi patented his 'wireless telegraph'.

Bose later turned his attention to plant life, plants being considered unresponsive in view of their lack of a nervous system. When he chloroformed plants Bose discovered that they were anaesthetised just as animals were, but recovered with removal of the chloroform just as we do. He experimented with carrots and turnips and found that they became as fatigued by persistent stimulation as we are. This was most obvious in the sensitive mimosa, but apparently all plants were similarly affected in greater or lesser degree. The following description appeared in the journal *Nation*:

> In a room near Maida Vale there is an unfortunate carrot strapped to the table of an unlicensed vivisector. Wires pass through two glass tubes full of a white substance,

they are like two legs, whose feet are buried in the flesh of the carrot. When the vegetable is pinched with a pair of forceps, it winces. It is so strapped that its electric shudder of pain pulls the long arm of a very delicate lever which actuates a tiny mirror. This cuts a beam of light on the frieze at the other end of the room, and thus enormously exaggerates the tremor of the carrot. A pinch near the right-hand tube sends the beam seven or eight feet to the right, and a stab near the other wire sends it far to the left. Thus can science reveal the feelings of even so stolid a vegetable as the carrot.

Bose started out as a penniless scientist with an ill-equipped, primitive laboratory in Calcutta. Like most radical discoverers he was ridiculed and misrepresented over a period of twenty years, usually by fellow scientists. Repeatedly he proved them wrong and found the support not only of Lord Rayleigh but also of Sir Oliver Lodge, Julian Huxley and Sir Charles Sherrington, president of the Royal Society. As usual it is the little man, the run-of-the-mill scientist who cannot abide radical discovery. Bose was definitely not of their company.

Do plants respond to sound? Most research on this appears to have been done in the United States. Scientists at the University of North Carolina have found that subjecting turnips to the excruciating sound of 100 decibels caused them to sprout much faster than others left silently in the ground. Since this is roughly the level of sound produced by a large plane taking off at an airport, most turnips, however, will have to do without it. Nevertheless plants do respond to milder stimulation. It has been discovered, again in the United States, that they are susceptible to music. Different kinds of music have been repeatedly played to such plants as radishes, geraniums and African violets. Plants do not respond equally to different kinds of music. They discriminate. 'Rock' music they turn away from. Apparently the heavy percussion is too much for them. Classical music, however, attracts them, string instruments best of all. Gourds, cucumbers and pumpkins responded well to the music of Beethoven, Brahms, Haydn and Schubert. Bach was also attractive to them. However, the sort of music that really got them on the move, drawing them towards the source of the music, was that of the Indian sitar played by Ravi Shankar.

May not then plants also respond to the human voice? All things considered, talk is a form of music. It has pitch and tone, piano and forte, crescendo and decrescendo, also timbre. It can be spoken con brio or adagio. What it may lack in emotion depends upon the speaker. Perhaps Prince Charles was not so ridiculous in talking to plants. The balance of popular credibility is heavily weighted in favour of the insensitivity of plants. So indeed was it to Sir Jagadish Bose, until he started subjecting them to experiment and found, after persistent hostility from fellow scientists, that they did in fact respond sensitively to stimuli.

Function Without Structure

We have been dealing with patterns and structures. Not everything has a recognisable pattern, though it helps us to understand it if it has. One patternless, structureless field of enquiry is that of parapsychology and extra-sensory perception – ESP. I myself have had little personal experience but I will introduce the subject by relating it to personal experience – such as it was. I have, for some years, had fortunate 'hunches' from time to time which turn out to be fruitful or 'just what I was looking for' – a sort of 'serendipity', which I imagine is not too unusual. It seemed to come into play mostly when I was looking up a reference in one of my books. The volume would open at the page I was looking for or it fell on the floor open at the required page. This happened so frequently that I almost took it as normal. There were one or two other instances, however, which could scarcely be regarded as normal.

My wife and I lived for forty-five years in an old cottage in Hampstead, London. It had been owned previously by George du Maurier, the author of *Trilby*, and he had installed his coachman in it. It was situated in The Mount (formerly Silver Street), just off the upper part of Heath Street. It had three floors and several small rooms. One morning, on waking, I went into the bathroom and was dumbstruck to find two turds in the bath. They were small and could, I suppose, have been deposited by a dog or cat. We had neither dog nor cat, nor did our neighbours. Both the bathroom door and window were closed. The following night I made sure that both door and window were firmly shut. Next morning on going into the bathroom I was confronted with a repetition of the previous day – again two turds in the bath. It was tempting to think that whatever had done the foul deed could not only count but probably had a sense of humour. It never occurred again. Nor did we ever find an answer to it.

At that time my wife was writing fairly regularly for the *New Statesman* and we used to have it delivered to the house. One day our copy was accompanied by an edition of *Izvestia*, which we had not ordered and would never have thought of ordering. Since it had come on the same day as 'The Staggers', and indeed with it, we wondered whether there could be any connection. My wife rang Tony Howard, the then editor of the *New Statesman*. He declared himself nonplussed and could give no explanation. If it happened again, would we tell him and he would make enquiries? As far as I can remember the *New Statesman* was sent to us from some distributing centre in, I think, High Wycombe. Perhaps it was also a centre for the distribution of *Izvestia* and there had been some mistake. So far nothing particularly unnatural, just some mistake in distribution. However, I am able to read simple Russian and I looked at the date on the copy of *Izvestia*. It was dated the same day, the day of its arrival. How, I wondered, could a paper published in Moscow get to High Wycombe and then on to us in apparently no time at all? It never occurred again, nor did we ever get an answer.

It occurred to me that perhaps certain areas might attract unusual happenings, a sort of local haunting, what the Germans call an 'ortsgebundene Spuk'. Our next-door neighbour – both our houses backed onto Money's Yard – was an architect and town-planner. She told us that as a girl she had experienced poltergeist phenomena. A breakfast tray had been dashed out of her hands. Apart from the above I have no other personal record of psychic or extra-sensory happenings. My wife Audrey, however, once had a spate of Ouija-boarding and table-rapping but got so scared at the results that afterwards she would have nothing to do with anything she considered unnatural.

I doubt whether ESP can be explained in terms of physical science, nor of logic, nor of mathematics. These are instruments for interpreting life in a way the rational mind can understand. ESP, however, is not a stable construct. It is fluid, elusive. It is function without structure. Trying to get a grip on it is like trying to collect water in a sieve or blood in a pair of forceps. There seems to me only one way of coming to any sort of grips with it; that is to experience it. To explain it is beyond our reach. However, this does not mean we should not try. We can perhaps get nearer a solution of the enigma even if a complete answer eludes us. In one sense it is like electricity. It works but no one can actually explain what it is. For centuries even its existence was unknown, though, if science is right, it must have been there.

In parapsychology, maps of the territory are like primitive maps in which the perimeter is not filled in. One encounters Dante's 'selva oscura', a wilderness, or more likely the legend 'Here be Dragons'. Sensible, rational people keep to the known, marked highways. Only fools and cranks go dragon hunting. Nevertheless a number of scientists and academics have so ventured, though the majority, the man in the street and those who value their reputation or respectability, have preferred to stick to what they know and can see and touch. They are careful not to be numbered among the gullible.

It is a disconcerting aspect of human nature, however, that those not prepared to stick their necks out or be taken for fools rarely make great discoveries or indeed any discoveries at all. Prudently they obey the rules, do not 'rock the boat' and 'do not suffer fools gladly'. Not a recipe, surely, for Einsteins or Galileos, nor even for parapsychologists. There may be safety in numbers, in the known and in the well-tried, but if venture had never overcome prudence we should all no doubt be still in the Stone Age.

Among those prepared to stick their necks out have been the following: Sir Oliver Lodge, Professor Gilbert Murray, William James, C. D. Broad, L. L. Vasiliev, Upton Sinclair, Rosalind Heywood, Gardner Murphy, Henry Margenau, C. G. Jung, Sir Alister Hardy and Francis Huxley. In addition Dr. John Beloff at Edinburgh University and Dr. J. B. Rhine of Duke University have conducted experiments in this field, the latter's achieving worldwide recognition. Of the above, Lodge, Gardner Murphy, Huxley and Hardy were scientists. Vasiliev was a Russian scientist in the Soviet Union, actively interested in parapsychology, Huxley was an anthropologist and Hardy a zoologist. C. D. Broad was a philosopher and William James both a philosopher and psychologist. Henry Margenau, another American, was Professor of Physics at Yale. The two writers Upton Sinclair and Rosalind Heywood both wrote in support of parapsychology, the latter with great insight and experience. Finally Professor Gilbert Murray, a noted Oxford classicist and Regius Professor of Greek, became president of The Society for Psychical Research.

This was by no means all. There were several others of equal or almost equal eminence but, compared with the vast army of academic sceptics, a drop in the ocean. Most, if not all, of the above are now dead, the problem of parapsychology still unresolved. Nor do I see any marked enthusiasm on the part of the majority of scientists to pursue what they would evidently rather not pursue. I remain convinced, however, that it will not go away and the opening up of the scientific field due to quantum theory could well provide a way through. In the now dying age of materialism, parapsychology was not only seen as an absurdity; it was a patent impossibility. With quantum theory, who knows, for quantum is itself on the edge of the parapsychological.

Whenever there is a possibility of a new science, a fresh source of knowledge, a radical break with tradition, there crops up, inevitably, a division of attitude. One side is largely manned by amateurs, the other by professionals. Most breaks with tradition have been instigated by amateurs while the defenders of tradition have normally been professionals. The former have, they think, much to gain and little to lose, the latter much to lose and nothing to gain. Professionals are often amateurs who have converted their love into a law and then cemented it in. Most advances in knowledge have been made by amateurs – people who loved knowledge, sought wisdom – philosophers. Science (Lat. 'scio' to know. Gk. 'epistēmē') was originally a branch of philosophy. The pupils of such philosophers then became academicians, professionals in schools and academies, like the Sophists before them. Socrates and Plato were amateurs, the one a street wiseacre the other a story-teller who was rather good at counting and who set up an 'Academy' of his own. One of his pupils, Aristotle, although he became a professional, was unlike any other before or since due in part, no doubt, to the myths and mathematics of his master.

Look back over history. Christ was an amateur, his Church a professional establishment, or at least it became one. Goethe was an amateur. Professional scientists paid him little attention. Baruch de Spinoza, a lens-grinder who became a philosopher, was also an amateur. So was Herbert Spencer. Michael Faraday was another. A journeyman bookbinder, he became a physicist and chemist, proposed the idea of magnetic 'lines of force' and developed the first electric generator. Even if one is a professional but goes one's own way one is, to some extent, an outsider. The establishment does not like being destabilised. It was not only the Church that pilloried Galileo but his fellow scientists also. Similarly with Einstein: scientific societies were set up in Germany to confute him. As for Copernicus, it was two hundred years before most professional astronomers could be persuaded that the earth went round the sun and that his *De Revolutionibus Orbium Caelestium* could be relied upon.

It appears to be much the same with parapsychology. Few professionals will touch it, for they fear their professionalism will be at stake and, with that, their reputation. For radical discovery to take place one has to do more than obey the rules. One may have to break them.

Morality

How did we get the idea that some things were right, others wrong? Animals do not labour under this ethical burden, which is quite alien to them. A dog snapping at a postman does not think it is doing anything wrong. Ideas of right and wrong appear to surface at a certain level of consciousness which human beings have attained and animals have not. Is there an ethical structure and, if so, how does it come into being? Is it innate or is it learned or imposed from outside by authority, whether parental or otherwise? Some, including C. G. Jung, come out in favour of an inborn code of morality. Others claim that we are essentially not immoral but amoral, and that unless we are taught it we have no sense of right or wrong.

The truth, as often, lies surely somewhere between the two. At one end of the spectrum lies perfection or truth; at the other imperfection – falsehood. To those who believe the sense of morality is innate, conscience moves up and down on a sort of internal staircase. It is aware of what is right, at the top of the staircase, but fails to reach it. To the believer that morality is not innate and has to be inculcated by others, the ethical staircase is not naturally felt but is seen as an imposition by authority. It may get assimilated and become part of one's nature while nevertheless still seen as an alien structure. Moreover, what is often a grey area tends to be seen as stark black or white, as if there were no intervening gradations between pure good and utter evil.

Both the innate and contingent versions can be seen as occupying the vertical and horizontal axes of Cassirer's cruciform structure which we have dealt with elsewhere. I was interested to see that the analytical psychologist Andrew Samuels in his *The Plural Psyche* also makes use of this vertical–horizontal framework. The innate version must, for obvious reasons, occupy the vertical axis, the

196

contingent version the horizontal. In Samuels's view the vertical split (superior–inferior), i.e., original morality, fuels the horizontal and becomes superimposed on the horizontal plane (self–other). The vertical aspect, the innate, is judgemental, and imposes its white–black, right–wrong on whatever happens to occupy the horizontal axis at the time; Samuels instances the Russia–America hostility conducted almost exclusively on black and white terms, each side *projecting* its own faults onto the other. According to Samuels innate morality has a 'fatal flaw' – its 'obsession with the superior–inferior dynamic' and is not enough for leading a moral life. But is, I wonder, the imposed version itself sufficient for the purpose? In actual life both versions in concert rarely appear to meet that requirement.

Ethics represents a constraint on behaviour externally, an urge to do better internally. It may start with an external 'must' and end with an internal 'ought', and it inevitably involves belief. If one doesn't believe, then the must is not listened to; the ought never develops. The external 'must' is usually represented by a parent or teacher. It is a voice of authority and may induce a sense of fear. If accepted, it is then interiorised and becomes internal authority. The child begins to control himself. The process is abetted by the fact that his friends and contemporaries have themselves been subject to a similar procedure and are beginning to establish their own moral code. Finally what started out as an external 'must' now stabilises as an internal 'ought', which he may well recognise as his 'conscience'. In contrast, the innate ethical process has the potentiality for evolving on its own, a sort of ethical 'entelechy' corresponding to physical and mental development.

The Dragon With Seven Heads
and Seven Crowns

Since the days of the Pythagoreans, structure, as in geometry, has always played a part in the understanding of
number. The numbers four, five and six, for instance, can
be seen as structures – the square, the pentagon and the
hexagon. The number seven, however, can only be seen
as a structure with difficulty, if at all. The number seven is
an oddity. With the exception of seven all numbers up to
and including ten if divided into the 360 degrees of the
circle result in a whole number. Seven bucks the trend
and falls out of line. When 360 degrees is divided by
seven we get 51.42857142857 ... and so on to infinity.
There are, one remembers, 52 weeks in the year and seven
days a week. Seven has an irrational, almost otherworldly
aspect about it. Why should a week have seven days? It
seems an odd number to choose unless there was some
mathematical reason or esoteric significance attached to it.
Mathematically it would seem to imply a rejection of
reason, a cult of irrationality, of incertitude, perhaps even
an intimation of chaos, a reminder that we were not just
programmed, mechanical robots even if we behaved as if
we were. There was something more to us, and perhaps
the number seven stood for it. Perhaps it was this aspect
that persuaded our ancient, and no doubt religious,
chronographers that the seventh day, the Sabbath, should
be a holy one. They enshrined the number seven in their
historico-mythology. Seven times seven or forty-nine was,
according to the Tibetan Book of the Dead, *The Bardo
Thodol*, the number of days the dead spent in the 'Bardo'
or limbo before being reincarnated. The number forty-
nine, seven times seven, is again the result of seven
divided by 0.142857, the recurring decimal mentioned
above. Further, any number divided by seven, with the
exception of fourteen, twenty-one, twenty-eight and other

multiples of seven will have the sequence 142857, 428571, 285714, 857142, 571428, 714285 as decimals, as if each digit sequentially removed itself one place in its impossible progress toward unattainable whole number.

The Book of Revelations went overboard with the number seven. We read of the seven churches of Asia, the seven golden candlesticks, the seven stars, the seven spirits of God, the seven lamps and the seven seals, the seven eyes of the seven spirits of God, the seven trumpets, the seven thunders, the dragon with seven heads and seven crowns, and so on, and so on. Let us not also forget the seven Christian virtues, the seven deadly sins and the seven wonders of the world. What is this strange connection between mathematics and the subconscious, or even the conscious? Does it have any meaning for a rationalist, materialist age? If we read Newton's *Optics* or look at a rainbow we see the seven colours of the spectrum. Newton was a religious man and not averse to esoteric knowledge. Again there are seven notes within the musical octave and we owe to Pythagoras, another religious scientist, the discovery of the musical intervals the 'fifth' and the 'fourth'. Both sight and sound, the most immaterial of the senses, incorporate the number seven in their structure. Perhaps if there is a meaning it is that of immateriality, which would accord with the mystico-religious aspect that history seems to have assigned to it.

Plato, who was interested in numbers, had a special feeling for the number seven and put it to practical effect. Seven was the highest prime number in the series 1–10. When he was devising the laws of The Republic he decided the optimum number of households in each 'polis' should be 5,040. Now 5,040 is the continued product of the integers from 1 to 7 ($1 \times 2 \times 3 \times 4 \times 5 \times 6 \times 7 = 5040$) and is obviously also divisible by every number up to ten. It is also divisible by twelve, thus relating households to divisions of the polis and the seasons and months of the year. We have then the seven days of the week, the four seasons (each of three months) of the year, and the 360 degree circle of the earth's rotation round the sun ($360 = 30 \times 12$ or 36×10). The Republic was a piece of clockwork as well as a geometrical design and a social arithmetical assignment.

The World as Respiration and Digestion

Our world of appearances we can regard as structure. A subtle, alluring, beautiful, astonishing structure and, at the same time, a cruel, bitter, tormenting and ruthless one. Appearances are inevitably dual. If we have good, there must also be bad, beauty is balanced by disfigurement, the hot by the cold, the light by the dark. In our apparent world we cannot escape its duality, which both enchants and torments us. It is a world of which we are both the creatures and the creators and it is two-faced because we too are two-faced. We and our world are part of each other. Without us our world does not exist. Without our world we do not exist. We hold each other up. That is a consequence of appearances, of phenomena. It is a sort of confidence trick but, in addition, a meaningful metaphor. The metaphor is there for us to read, to interpret, to learn. For what object? To get beyond the pattern of appearance into reality, beyond the phenomena to the noumenon, to seek The One through The Many. The seeking is the function for which the appearances are the structure. The whole is a pattern of 'Becoming'.

Our world of appearances, however, is not an illusion. It is real enough – for us, for it is we who bring it about. Being part of it we are programmed to see it as it appears and we tailor it to our own measure, as it, in turn, cuts us to its cloth. We are, in effect, sewn into our world. We think we can stand outside it and examine it objectively. We can't. We think it is out there and we are in here. But we are in constant living exchange with it. At one moment the air is part of our environment, in the next, part of us, as we breathe it in. The same goes for what we eat and drink. One moment it is part of our environment, the next part of us. We have just had a meal. It is all there, staring us in the face, at the end of our fingertips, under our feet, assaulting our ears. Bertrand Russell claimed that our bodies were just as much part of our environment as tables and chairs were. It is all part of us and we cannot recognise it.

Though we breathe in the world at every breath, then exhale it, ingest and excrete it every day, it is not merely a convenient symbiosis; it is essential, like a new-born baby linked by an umbilical cord with its mother. But we behave as if we were independent beings capable of objective thought, of action which has no consequences for the life of others. Neither galaxies nor sub-atomic particles are independent, not from each other, nor even from us. We are all part of the cosmic soup, breathing, ingesting, excreting, appreciating, meeting, avoiding, creating destroying those parts of our world with which we appear to come into contact. The *bacillus coli* in our gut does much the same and its apparent world is even more restricted than ours. The symbiosis, however, is not confined to our immediate environment. It embraces all.

No one knows what lies behind or beyond appearances. Religion has attempted to storm the battlements of unknowing, with scant success. Mystics have claimed to have breached the wall but since what they experienced was ineffable they have been unable to describe it. Science, which does not believe that anything lies beyond appearances, has made no attempt. It is enmeshed in a spider's web of appearances and maintains that that is all there is. What it cannot measure, what it cannot count, cannot be. Appearance is all. Plato wrote of saving appearances *sōzein ta phainomena*. We are still trying to do it, for we are still in Plato's 'Cave' and no amount of science, technology and religious bumbledom will get us out of it. Shackled like the prisoners in the cave, we cannot even turn round but are forced to watch the shadows on the wall in front, mistaking them for reality. The cave is our world, just as our gut, our digestive tract is the apparent world of the *bacillus coli*. To penetrate the metaphor, a metanoia, a fundamental change of mind, is imperative, and these, like paradigm shifts in science, are upsetting and usually vigorously opposed.

It is suggested that a first step in the grammar and syntax of metaphorical interpretation might be an enquiry into the structure and function of appearances. It is useful to have a pattern, however primitive. This is only a primer. Further investigation is up to the reader.

Reaching Beyond Time

We have been talking of structure and function, the former a condition of space, the latter of time. Time appears more elusive than space. We cannot hear, see or touch time. Physically we experience it in what we recognise as change. Mentally we appreciate it through the immediacy of present experience, through memory of the past and through anticipation of the future. Time is fluid. It flows from past to present to future, from the 'no longer' to the 'not yet'. It also appears to flow backward since the future in due course becomes the present and later still the past. Time is often contrasted with eternity. 'Tempora mutantur' – times change. Eternity, however, does not. There is no past or future in eternity. It is not an extension of time to infinity. Eternity is the eternal present. It is with us *here and now*. It is outside time. Unlike time it is no longer Becoming. It is Being.

We are living in time and eternity at once – now. We spin time out of ourselves as a spider spins its web, while being at the same time caught up in it. The spinning is the function, the web the structure. We create, and are ensnared by, both. There is another part of us, however, which is not subject to time, nor created by it. It is essentially neither physical nor mental and, for want of a better word, is known as the spirit. The spirit is beyond time. It rests in eternity, in the eternal 'now' and the ubiquitous 'here'. When we die our physical and mental existence ceases, and time with it, since time does not exist without our experience. What, we are told, was once us is now in eternity though *we* are no longer there to experience it, since to experience it would involve bringing in not only time but our mental and physical capacity for experience, which with death we have sloughed off.

The spirit is bodyless, mindless, spaceless, timeless. How does one know this? One doesn't know how. It is an

203

ancient assumption to which many if not most religions appear to subscribe. Is my spirit any different from yours? Apparently no. The root of all is the same. But there are branches. And what branches from the trunk is, to some, the soul. The soul is an intermediary between mind and spirit. It has one foot in time, the other in eternity, one foot in the here, the other in the not-here or no-where. It is a go-between uniting the individual with The All, integrating the part into the whole. In science, analogously, it is the role of mathematics. The soul is considered to carry with it a distillation of the accumulated experience of the individual and brings it into association with the comprehension of The All. The spirit does not experience. It just *is*. If there is any life after death, e.g., the experiencing of anything whatever, whether material, such as in reincarnation, or immaterial, such as 'geistlich' or ghostly, then the quality of such rebirth, since as an experience it must have a quality, would seem to depend on the condition of the soul.

There is a pertinent passage which Professor W. T. Stace has adapted from Heinrich Zimmer's *Philosophies of India* (1951):

The saints set forth in the Great Ferryboat which is to carry them from the hither shore of this world across the river of Samsara to the far shore which is Nirvana. As they proceed, the shore which they are leaving grows fainter and fainter until it disappears in the mist, the far shore at the same time slowly arising on their vision. The Great Ferryboat arrives and the saints disembark. But for them, now in Nirvana, there are no longer any distinctions and therefore there is no distinction between Nirvana and non-Nirvana, this world and the next, the hither shore and the far shore. There is not, and there never was, any hither shore from which they set out; there never was any ferryboat or any passengers or any Nirvana, or any saints who have entered Nirvana. Nirvana too is nothing, the Void.

Professor Stace points out that the meaning of the paradox is not that there is no Nirvana, no Primal Being, no Universal Self. What it means is that they are imcomprehensible to the logical understanding, and that even to call them 'paradoxical' is to apply to them a logical category which misrepresents them, and that even to say 'they are' or 'they are not' is only to utter vain words about the Unutterable.

We are treading unknown territory, the nebulous realm of mysticism, a realm which to the hard-headed man in the street, no less than to the materialist scientist, does not and cannot exist. Yet no less a rational thinker than Bertrand Russell claimed that 'the greatest men who have been philosophers have felt the need of both science and mysticism' and that 'this emotion – mysticism – is the inspirer of whatever is best in man'. One cannot analyse mysticism. Unlike reason it is elusive and unsplittable. Grasping it, it escapes us. Trying to pin down the unpinnable with the sharp instrument of logic is a hopeless and unattainable task. The Pythagoreans divided the world into 'the limited' (*to peras*) and 'the unlimited' (*to apeiron*). Reason belongs to the limited world which is, of course, also the world of appearances. Mysticism belongs to the unlimited, the eternal world of Being, as Plato, Meister Eckhart and William Blake well knew. Reason is multiple. Mysticism is single. There are no distinctions in The One, not between object and object, nor between subject and object. There is only the seamless, indestructible, limitless One.

One, Two, Three ... Infinity

The above title is that of a book by the Nobel prizewinning physicist George Gamow. However, this piece is not about physics but what underlies physics – mathematics. The science of mathematics has long been a puzzle to mathematicians – what is it, how does it come about, is it man-made or does it arise from nature? Like electricity we don't have to know exactly what it is before we can use it. It works whatever we think of it. Practically speaking, if a tool does its job efficiently it is of minor importance who made it or of what it is made. But suppose the tool is sufficiently flexible and comprehensive to be applicable to several jobs, perhaps all jobs, even to the extent of under-lying everything that is. Perhaps then we should want to know, not so much of what it can do – we are aware of that – but of its origins, how it arose, and of its essential nature.

An adequate answer is probably unobtainable. There are some subjects which elude all attempts at solution and this is probably one of them. All I will attempt to do here is to take a few stochastic shots at a target whose bull's-eye is unobtainable or perhaps, to all intents and pur-poses, does not exist. It seems to me that mathematics is neither wholly a property of mind, nor of matter, e.g., nature. it partakes of both. It is a 'go-between'. It is neu-tral. Like mercury it is capable of producing an amalgam, or like an enzyme, effecting change without itself being changed. As a go-between it may act as a link between opposites or apparent incompatibles, say between the ideal and the real, the universal and the particular. In this respect it may resemble Aristotle's 'potentia', a sort of limbo of possibility between two extremes.

Like time and space mathematics is a co-ordinating system measuring both, first apparently separating them and then uniting them in a space–time continuum.

Metaphorically it is at once wave-like and corpuscular, analogic and digital. The word 'mathēma' in Greek meant 'learning' and the aim of learning 'knowledge'. It was of neutral gender (*to mathēma*) semantically and semiotically a go-between. Symbolically it is associated with the Greek god Hermes (Lat. Mercury), again a go-between, a neutral, as in 'hermaphrodite' and in the word 'hermeneus' a translator, or 'hermeneutics' the art of interpretation, which is precisely its function as a key to knowledge.

The hermaphrodite nature of mathematics is reflected in the division between rational and irrational. There are, for example, irrational numbers and the concept of infinity, both of which take mathematics into 'another world'. Moreover, if the structure of mathematics is axiomatic its function is often of an intuitive nature, even paradoxical or perverse rather than rational. Many great mathematicians have developed theorems which they can neither explain nor prove, but which have nevertheless furthered the science. As befits its Janusface, mathematics is the arena in which both the rational and irrational joust for precedence. Professional mathematicians tend to side with the rational, axiomatic aspect. Those who invent new geometries and theories have to venture beyond such rigid limits. Discovering that the structure is inadequate, they feel obliged to fracture it and break new ground or look at it again athwart searching for radically new avenues of approach. Some of the greatest mathematicians, such as Poincaré, are examples. Here intuition often plays an important part, for reasoning has its limits. It is perhaps not to be lightly dismissed that that great advocate of mathematics, Plato, was also, by many accounts, of mystical bent.

A name to play with in mathematics is Ramanujan. Mathematical truths are often discovered in a flash of insight, the numerical precedent seeming to have little to do with the abrupt and unexpected enlightenment, while the subsequent rational explanation is often unattainable. Ramanujan was perhaps the most astonishing example of intuitive mathematical discovery ever. He was born in India a century or more ago. He was not a highly educated man and did not even go to university, but when he died at the early age of thirty-two he left behind him four thousand mathematical formulas and in his last year produced more mathematical theories than most good mathematicians provide in a lifetime.

The point about the above is that his theorems were not just run-of-the-mill mathematics. Many of them defeated the best mathematicians then and since. Yet they appeared to just 'flow out of his brain'. Like Fermat's last theorem, they have resisted the attempts of others to fathom them for generations. The most rational of the sciences would also appear to be the most intuitive; the most objective is also the most subjective. The dichotomy underlying its unity goes deep and is apparently ubiquitous. Mathematics both separates and unites function and structure, time and space, energy and matter. It is the ghostly amalgam which fuses and holds everything together while it is also the separating factor which distinguishes the part from the whole. It is the intermediary, the 'tertium interveniens', the 'holy ghost' of the trinity of life. It has no material existence and is neither above nor below but between the universal and the particular, separating them but potentially uniting them. It is our conceptual paraclete. Mathematics embraces both infinite and finite. Without the infinite there would be no mathematics. Without the finite there would be no nature, no external world. Without the ideal there would be no theory, without the real, no fact. Mathematics both separates (either-or) and unites them (both-and). One is left with the impression that it arises from the implicit realisation that man and his universe are one in spite of the apparent severance.

Mathematics can be proved. Quod erat demonstrandum. Nothing else, not even logic, can be so rigidly, axiomatically, proven. In humanity and nature, however, there is only approximation, not exactitude. Life must have room for manoeuvre, to err, to diverge, to progress and develop. It therefore has to break, or leak through the frozen axiomatic structure of mathematics. The ice-cold perfection of the ideal melts in the warmth of living nature. Yet the ideal is essential as an objective measure in the subjectivity of life.

In our evolving, apparent world all is in flux and, to the extent that mathematics penetrates it, it too may evolve. It can grow with our understanding of it as an instrument of Being may penetrate our world of Becoming. As we evolve, so does our understanding of mathematics. The geometry of Euclid may have been seen as perfect, complete, but since then we have had new geometries, those of Riemann, Bolyai, Lobachevsky and others. They all work, just as Euclid still works for fields in which it is appropriate. Mathematics is not the 'ghost in the machine'; it is the ghost behind the emergence of life. It is an immaterial substrate presenting us with a framework of correlates and conceptual 'ordering operators' (Pauli). It is neither the child of man nor of nature but of the union of both. Mathematics both unites and divides. It divides for information but unites for understanding, as also does the mind. Reductionism and holism are aspects of its limitations.

Some hint of the above seems to have registered in the last days of the Roman Empire. Boethius, who was the last great Roman to understand Greek and who translated Aristotle, also had a Pythagorean view of music and mathematics. He divided music into three types – 'musica mundana', the harmony of the spheres, 'musica humana', the harmony of the human soul and body, and 'musica instrumentalis', the actual playing of music. The first two related to Pythagoras's mathematico-musical experiments and his claimed 'music of the spheres', which we have touched on elsewhere. Mathematics and music were subtly interwoven in human experience.

In the medieval university, the 'studium generale', study was divided seven-fold and again into three and four, the 'Trivium' and the 'Quadrivium'. Music was assigned to the Quadrivium, together with arithmetic, geometry and astronomy, its mathematical relevance being duly recognised. Music was regarded as a kind of set of repetitive measures resulting in harmony, much as a set of arithmetical figures may result in an equation. For this and other reasons it was assigned a place in the Quadrivium. In the medieval mind the mathematical harmony manifested itself not only in sound but also externally in human artifacts. The great Gothic cathedrals, for instance, were conceived as music in stone, musical proportions being incorporated in their architecture, a form of musical mathematics. In the fifteenth and sixteenth centuries many buildings, especially in Italy, incorporated such proportions in their architecture. Andrea Palladio and Leone Battista Alberti were two of the architects who incorporated music in stone.

We can see here an alliance between cerebral mathematics and sensual appreciation resulting in harmonious external structure, with music seen as a sensual aspect of mathematics. One can take the relationship further, for even such materialistic considerations as proportions of the musical scale, the distances between the black and white notes on a piano keyboard or those between the frets of a guitar correspond to the Fibonacci Series in mathematics. Rhythm, proportion and measure appear to permeate more thoroughly than we suspect not only ourselves but nature herself – the growth of plants, the spiralling of shells and of the horns and claws of animals, the helical forms of tornadoes and whirlpools, even the shape of galaxies, all of which correspond with that curiosity of mathematics, the logarithmic spiral, not, it is true, accurately, for in nature nothing is accurate, but near enough to be unmistakable. Appearances always stray a little from the universal ideal, as Plato was well aware.

Are there other mathematical relationships of which we should take note? Undoubtedly and ubiquitously. I will mention just one: the relationship between body and mind involving response to stimuli. In his two-volume *Elemente der Psychophysik* the German philosopher and physicist Gustav Fechner made public his discovery that there is a mathematical relationship between the intensity of a stimulus and that of its response – Fechner's Law, or alternatively the Weber–Fechner Law. This law stated that the intensity of the sensation was proportional to the logarithm of the stimulus, and Fechner regarded it as basic to an understanding of the relationship between body and mind. Wherever one looks, it is difficult not to recognise the ubiquitous role of mathematics. It is a major key to understanding but we still do not really understand just what mathematics is. A lack of understanding, however, seems to be no bar to manipulation. It works and we make it work. If only we could understand, perhaps a new world might open up to us.

Aggression

In another chapter the subject of aggression was touched on in connection with a survey of types of people most likely to aspire, or succumb, to its seductive charms. Is there a recognisable structure to aggression? Moreover, is it an inherited instinct or something we learn to exercise? The latter question has occupied the minds of a number of ethologists. On a professional level we may note Konrad Lorenz and Niko Tinbergen, while on a more popular level we have Robert Ardrey (*African Genesis*) and Desmond Morris (*The Naked Ape*). There are, of course, others, but those mentioned will do for our purpose. These four have all assumed that aggression is a basic instinct not only in animals but in human beings also, and that as a natural consequence we have violence between individuals, riots on the social scale and wars on the national scale. We are, like the animals they have studied, instinctive, aggressive fighters. It would appear that if they are right, we are doomed to fight, to kill, to murder, to go to war for ever. There is no point in trying to master our aggression. It is inbuilt, part of us. Any attempts to build a fair, equitable and peaceful society are a waste of time. We cannot do anything ourselves. We are passive subjects of our instincts.

This, while perhaps rather pessimistic on the one hand, could be seen as a blessing on the other. It relieves us of a load of guilt. We are no longer responsible for what we do. If we murder someone, it is human, part of our nature. We cannot be blamed for what is natural to us. This, possibly, is why *The Naked Ape* became such a popular success. This belief was also not new. It had been fostered by Freud and others and by the 'social Darwinism' that followed the publication of *The Origin of Species*. 'Nature red in tooth and claw' was a popular phrase for describing the instinct of an aggression too powerful for us to master. If we wanted proof we had only to observe the tiger, the wolf, the shark or birds of prey, for were we not, as Darwin made clear to us, descended from animals too? As humans, more evolved than animals, our instincts were even more murderous. The tiger and the wolf killed when hungry. They had to in order to live. We on the other hand could kill when we were sated, when we just did not like someone, when we wanted his land, his money or his wife. We and others of our tribe or nation could kill thousands and, in a war, millions. Compared with us the tiger and the shark were puny aggressors, their bloody teeth producing no more than gnat-bites. Again, unlike the tiger and shark, we killed each other – other humans. Animals, it seems, are poor aggressors. Unlike us they only killed other species, not their own. We have gone much further and can, it appears, actually enjoy killing. Since it was all instinctive, or as we would probably now say 'all in the genes', we were not responsible. In the dock we could say, 'not guilty, your Honour, I was programmed to do it'.

Are the instincts we are told we inherited from our ancestors, from the great apes, from animal life in general, really so inherited? What are instincts? Some have questioned whether there are such things as instincts at all. We assume, perhaps too early, that we know the answers. Then again, are animal instincts comparable with ours? What proof have we? The ground is not as firm as some would have it. Lorenz Tinbergen, for instance, conducted his researches largely on birds, e.g., geese, in captivity, not leading a normal existence in the wild. Actions while in captivity are not the same as those in the wild. That epitome of aggression, the rat, is in the wild not an outstandingly aggressive creature but when caged and crowded with others it can easily become so. So, I would suspect, could I. But that is due not to inherited aggressiveness but to environmental coercion. There is a 'density tolerance' in crowding, both in time and space. People in densely occupied streets or slums are much more inclined to violence than those in leafy suburbs or the countryside. There are crowds and crowds, each having its own distinctive pattern depending on circumstance, as Elias Canetti in his *Crowds and Power* has analysed. Human beings also have the added complication of invented environments, television, video games and so on, many of which are often very violent indeed. Violence breeds violence and feeds violence, and many an aggressive act has mirrored its instigator on television. From the above one gets the impression that aggression is learned or copied rather than innate. Those who deny this have mostly carried out their researches not in the wild but in captivity, where aggression is generally most noticeable. Those who have actually observed animals in their wild state have come to a different conclusion. Kropotkin in his book *Mutual Aid* presents us with a very different picture, of mutual help rather than of aggression. Jane Goodall, who lived with chimpanzees in Tanzania and the Congo, records the friendliness and helpfulness of chimps. Among them real aggression was very rare, though sometimes simulated, the simulation being perfectly understood for what it was. Other writers, Geoffrey Gorer, the zoologist Sir Solly Zuckerman and the anthropologist Ashley Montagu, have come to similar conclusions.

But what exactly is aggression? It is, surely, an extrapolation, a variation or a misapplication of a more basic impulse – energy itself. No one can deny the existence of energy or that it is innate. Energy, however, feeds several offshoots of which we can make narrower and more particular use: limb movement, for instance, lifting, carrying, gripping, gesticulation, walking and so on. Aggression is just one path that energy may take, but unlike energy it is not innate. It may, or may not, arise as the result of environmental pressure of some kind or other – too many rats crowded into a cage. It may also be learned or copied. Violence on television may, for instance, lead the viewer to copy it in life. Living in a violent community may lead to even a gentle person becoming violent. It is difficult, if not impossible, to become aggressive without an object to aggress, and that is provided by the milieu, other people, the outside world, not by instinct. Our environment may be material, social, or even psychological, since what we experience is part of our inner environment. And since our own body is also part of our environment, aggression can result in self-mutilation or suicide.

Our environment provides the structure for the expression of energy, stamps it with a certain character derived from the milieu within which it operates. Aggression is the result of the combination impulse–structure, instinct–environment. The structure guides and maybe twists or warps the flow of energy, and may, in the process, become warped itself. We are not born to kill. We learn from circumstance to do it. A birth in favourable circumstances could do much to curb aggression.

Spinning the Periphery Around the Centre

Beyond the pale of appearances, of space and time, what can be the reality? Beyond movement there must be stillness, beyond Becoming there surely must be Being to which Becoming aspires. One can envisage a still centre and a perimeter capable of expansion. At the centre is the origin and end of everything. It is always there, beyond time and space, eternally in the present moment, the here and now. One can imagine it as an infinitisimal point, what in Indian philosophy is called 'Bindu'. One can imagine this Nothing of a point as pure spirit, nameless, featureless, placeless, timeless. The point, however, has potentiality. It can spread and evolve towards a non-existent perimeter. As it spreads it takes on a primitive aspect of space and time, for movement is not possible without space-time. Both space and time are latent in the potentiality. As it expands it begins to diversify, becomes more complicated and multiform. The spirit evolves, taking on an aspect of life. It engenders an 'élan vital' which in turn impregnates every living organism (function energising structure). As in embryology and biological evolution it expands, diversifies and advances whatever it encounters. At the same time it leaves the noumenal world and enters our phenomenal world of appearances. We can now experience through reason and our sensory-motor equipment what was hidden to us before except through intuition, illumination or revelation, which the phenomenal world does not admit. We are now in territory available to science which is ever striving to attain the periphery and, if possible, extend it still further, with reductionism its most favoured method, increasingly dividing and splitting up an already complicated world.

Lack of movement – rest – has no opposition within itself. However, outside itself its opposite is motion. Motion has also an opposition within itself. In the present

216

instance motion outward toward the perimeter is mirrored by a movement toward the centre, a movement toward interconnection, integration and wholeness, the perimeter striving to get back to the centre. Spirit descending into matter moves outward. Matter striving toward spirit moves inward – an involutionary movement. In his book *Wholeness and the Implicate Order* the physicist David Bohm gives a physical illustration of this outward-inward movement. Suppose one has a cylindrical vessel filled with glycerine and within this place, a smaller cylinder. Then drop into the glycerine between the two cylinders a small droplet of ink. The droplet is not dispersed since the glycerine holds it together. If, however, one rotates one of the cylinders the drop of ink spreads out in the opposite direction to the rotation. It dwindles into a thin line and finally disappears altogether. The droplet is enfolded into the glycerine and is invisible, but the potentiality for its reconstitution is still there. If one rotates the cylinder back in the opposite direction the thin line begins to reappear and finally the droplet. So it is with the dispersion of the spirit in the ouward direction and the proliferation of life. Again, so it is with the reconstitution of the spirit in the inward direction and the return of life to its source. Science and technology move ever outward toward the perimeter, our world of appearances. It is called 'progress'. The opposite movement, from outer to inner, is individual and preferred by intuitives, the enlightened and mystics. They unite the part with the whole, The All with The One, Omega with Alpha, the creation to the creator.

In cosmic terms we can see the outward movement reflected in the evolution of the universe itself, which also, we are told, is expanding and diversifying. Is there, perhaps, a corresponding inward movement? Could there be a sort of alternating current, a 'Yin–Yang' reversal, a two-way pulsation, expanding and contracting like the 'breath of Brahma' which, one understands, lasts 4,320,000,000 years between each inspiration and expiration? However, unless rebirth or reincarnation is an option we are doomed never to know the answer and, since memory is untransmissible, not even then. Scientifically we can only guess.

Further, it should be remembered that such theories and mathematics relate only to our universe of appearances, a universe which we have constructed out of our unavoidably anthropocentric experience. If there are living beings from other planets or galaxies, they will have their own universes tailored to their own respective capacities for interpretation, as do our own dogs, cats or tapeworms. Scientists avoid this aspect of cosmology because there is no means of measuring it. But that does not excuse the non-recognition of their limitations.

We have described a centre and a periphery with both a centrifugal and a centripetal movement. There is also a rotational movement, the periphery spinning round the still centre. The centre is the 'eye' of the tornado, the whirlpool or vortex. The centre, The Void, The Godhead, or whatever one chooses to call it, for it has no name of itself, is always there, always the same, but the spiralling vortex changes. Other worlds may surface, appearance worlds like our own, together with other deaths and other rebirths, each with its rarer and denser matter, its structure, its logic, mathematics and life, which themselves evolve with the evolution of their respective worlds.

With the evolution of individual life comes the duality of pleasure and pain. With the devolution of spirit comes the duality of good and evil and the dubious blessing of free-will, for spirit forces ethical choices upon us which we would often rather not have. Spirit is to life as life is to matter. It evolves as life evolves, proliferates and complexifies in consciousness as life does in organisms. It is the ethical equivalent of life and gives meaning to an otherwise meaningless, purposeless drama, authorless, misunderstood, full of sound and fury, signifying nothing.

The Balance of Terrorism

Belief and disbelief are the accelerator and brake to everything we do, everything we can think of, even imagine. They are the springs and checks to life itself. When it comes to politics the scenario can reach frightening proportions. It can take form as war or peace, prosperity or starvation, the care or the abandonment of millions. Such vital questions are determined by people delegated by us to do so, governments. People themselves have little say. They are not educated to assess the issues and they are under constant propaganda to accept what their governments believe and these, in turn, are rarely better educated, or fitted, to judge such issues. In most cases it is a matter of the blind leading the blind. The led are led to believe their leaders and, in most cases, they do. In each country, when it appears, or is made to appear, that national sovereignty is threatened, the press and the media with few exceptions fall into line. The more acute the perceived crisis, the more 'patriotic' the response. Dissidents may be dismissed as cranks, labelled unpatriotic, or put under lock and key.

In wartime, it appears, people can be persuaded to believe almost anything. The advice of sceptics – never believe anything until it is officially denied – though salutary, stands little chance against the official propaganda to which people are subjected. Governments believe what they want to believe, and what they want to believe is seldom the truth. It is rather what will give them an advantage over other governments, 'enemy' or otherwise, or an economic advantage of some sort, or the need to keep their own people under control. There are few more effective ways of quelling internal unrest than that of exaggerating the threat of external danger, even that of invasion. In recent years the causes of war have reflected the need, or the greed, for oil, and where greed and economics are involved, to say nothing of a government's desire for self-preservation, lying is regarded not only as permissible but as virtually indispensable.

Never take a government at its word. Let us take the most powerful government the world has ever seen, that centred in Washington DC. It proclaims freedom, equality and democracy. The first and last sentences of Lincoln's Gettysburg Address could hardly be bettered in any national paean. As a nation the United States has high ideals. However, it seems to have difficulty in living up to such ideals in actual practice. Indeed, it almost seems to enjoy perverting them. Not long ago it was engaged in an attack on 'terrorism'. Two of its embassies in East Africa were bombed and the terrorists were assumed, but not proved, to be agents of some Islamic country. Washington's response was to attack a pharmaceutical factory in the Sudan and the hide-out in Afghanistan of the presumed author of the embassy bombings. In both cases many innocent people were killed or injured. Terrorism was met by terrorism.

The United States claims that a nation has a right to defend itself and such action is therefore justified. But the United States itself had not been attacked. It is the most powerful nation in the world and, at a distance of some eight thousand miles, reasonably free from attacks on its homeland. It did not even consult the United Nations as it should have done before taking such action. It took 'the law' into its own hands. While wanting to be accepted as 'world policeman', it put itself, without compunction, into the position of 'world outlaw'.

All nations tend to be less than even-handed in their use of the word 'terrorism'. The bombing of the American embassies *was* terrorism. The destruction by cruise missiles of targets in the Sudan and in Afghanistan from US ships in the Red Sea and the Persian Gulf was also terrorism, but not to the United States. To them it was a legitimate response. The United States, we are told, never indulges in terrorism. The word is reserved for its presumed enemies. Since the word is also used by its enemies against the United States or indeed by any nation against any other if it so suits the official stance, it amounts to little more than name-calling. This is a pity, for terrorism is a reality not confined to any nation or alignment of nations. It is a brutal weakness most have indulged in at some time or other down the ages.

When the United States talks of terrorism, has it, perhaps, forgotten the Vietnam War, the massacre of My Lai, the use of Agent Orange and napalm and the wanton destruction of hundreds of square miles of a poor oriental country? The United States was not being threatened. From their safe seats in a bomb-safe, napalm-safe country half the world away from the scene of conflict, successive governments in Washington derided the Vietnamese as 'gooks' and accused them of terrorism. The fact that in the end Vietnamese bicycles defeated American gun-ships is not mentioned and is decently shelved. Propriety must be observed and the word terrorism reserved for one's enemies.

The sorry history of American terrorism does not stop there. Have we forgotten the overthrow of the democratic government of Chile and the installation of the military regime of General Pinochet, all aided and abetted by the CIA, who helped to usher in a period of torture and the 'disappearance' or death of hundreds if not thousands? Have we forgotten American aid to the Greek Colonels and their murderous junta? Have we forgotten Colombia, Panama, Nicaragua, El Salvador, Cuba, the Bay of Pigs and the attempted assassination of Fidel Castro? In most cases they were attempts by the United States to replace governments that it did not like by right-wing governments that it did, at the cost of countless lives and, in the case of Cuba, with continuing sanctions.

The United States, of course, is not the only, nor the worst, offender in wielding the big stick. The Nazis under Hitler and the communists under Stalin were yet more destructive. Even the British, who like to think of themselves as a civilised and tolerant people, have a history of violence it would be difficult to equal. The British have fought more wars, conquered more territory and subdued more peoples than any other nation since history began. They have also driven, with other nations, hundreds of thousands into slavery. Now Britain, its teeth still not drawn, since it is up to the ears in armaments, finds itself nevertheless unable to finance any further depredations and looks to its imperial successor the United States to take its place, which the latter has only too willingly assumed. Apparently unable now to stand alone with its own homebred foreign policy, the British Government has repeatedly kow-towed to Washington. No one should, therefore, be surprised that the government should play lap-dog to Washington. It has been doing so for years.

The sad story is that it all depends on belief and, in many cases, mistaken belief. The Americans believe that the Arabs are terrorists and, in certain cases, they may well be right. The Arabs believe precisely the same about the Americans. Neither will admit that the other could possibly be right or itself wrong. Moreover, neither will accept to be judged by an impartial authority such as the United Nations. Both have gone a step beyond belief; they *know* they are right.

Belief when accepted as knowledge is an extremely dangerous concept. It confirms our worst suspicions. There is no going back to 'probably' or 'might be'. Possibility gives way to 'fact', and fact just *is*. There's no getting away from it – fact is final. One's mind is made up, the door to doubt closed. But what is this 'fact'? Is it as hard, impenetrable, ineluctable as it appears? Goethe was one who did not find it so. He came to the conclusion that 'everything factual depends on theory'. It was not the solid, indisputable thing it has been for so long assumed to be. A brave, perhaps foolhardy, assertion two centuries ago. But now quantum physics has come to Goethe's rescue. The hard facticity of a thing has been shown to be fallacious. In essence Goethe was right. Facts are no longer the solid reliable things we thought they were. They are even a bit fuzzy round the edges which, for people who see things precisely and all in black and white, is a bit disconcerting. So perhaps we can become sceptical about facts, as about everything else.

Can we persuade governments of this? Belief is positive, scepticism negative, and to most people the positive is usually preferable. Few people pride themselves on being negative. Belief is the accelerator, disbelief the brake, and governments, in common with most of us, like the think of themselves as positive, to feel power. The prospects for peace are thereby not helped. We could, perhaps, get people to question everything, especially everything authoritative, but could we ever get governments to question themselves? It seems unlikely. They have to be seen as firm and decisive, with their hand on the helm, their foot on the accelerator, their finger on the button, preferably the nuclear button; not for them the debilitating quality of doubt.

One trouble with terrorism and even more with war is that the perpetrators often escape. It seems to be always the poor, the helpless and deprived who most suffer. Perhaps this is one reason why war and terrorism flourish. It is rarely the well-upholstered, the jet-set, financiers and those with power that get caught. They have the money and the means of escape and generally danger areas are not within their jet-stream. They rarely even lose their money, which, if they are prudent, they have stacked away in remote tax-avoidance locations so that their less well-provided compatriots are unable to benefit from their expertise in milking the economy. The poor and deprived, however, have no such luck. They have to take whatever is coming to them. Perhaps if war and terrorism were to count as their first victims those in a position to start a war, those benefiting from it and those able to escape from it, then, possibly, we might have some hope of peace. However, in this ruthless, predatory and belligerent century, that would no doubt be crying for the moon.

What is the structure behind this inconjunction of opposites? It would appear to relate to Cassirer's vertical–horizontal framework. On the face of it war relates to the horizon. As we have seen, there are two cardinal versions of the concept of opposition: that of Heraclitus, Chuang-Tzu and Hegel, and on the other hand that of Aristotle. The former presents us with a harmony in contrariety, the latter with a contradiction. It is the latter which, down the centuries, has attracted our rulers, whereas the common people, given the choice, which of course they are never given, might well have opted for the former. But the rulers, as we have noted elsewhere, occupy not the horizontal but the vertical axis, the axis not of free discussion between equals or of choice, but that of command (upper pole) and obedience (lower pole). The vertical axis has, as it were, taken over and usurped the function of the horizontal, perverting the meaning of the latter. The vertical, essentially, is an internal, mental, within – the – individual ethical axis of better or worse. When, however, it is read as an outer, material structure relating not within the individual but between people, its better or worse becomes 'might is right'. The horizontal, ideally an external physical axis representing relationships on a basis of equality and justice between people or groups of people, itself becomes perverted by the usurpation of its significance by the perversion of the vertical. Class war could be interpreted in similar fashion.

Tea and Sympathy

Some years ago six people gathered together for tea in a house in north Wales. They were Bertrand Russell and his fourth wife Edith, an Anglican parson, the Rev. Michael Scott, a Naga chieftain by the name of Phizo, his daughter and myself. We were all having tea in Bertrand Russell's house, Plas Penrhyn, Penrhyndeudraeth. What could have brought such a mixed bag together: an atheist philosopher, an anti-apartheid priest formerly of Sophiatown, Johannesburg and a father and daughter from Nagaland on the northeast border of India? As for me, Michael Scott was an old friend who had persuaded me to come with him. He was also an old friend of Russell's. A pretty diverse if not eccentric lot, one might think.

What brought us all together, however, was Jawarhalal Nehru. Both Russell and Scott knew Nehru well. Scott, in a fairly tempestuous life, had spent some time in India and was on friendly terms with Nehru, while Russell had also known him personally. The trouble was, Nehru had plans to take over Nagaland and incorporate it into India. The Nagas, represented by Phizo, wished to remain independent, and Scott, who had been to Nagaland and sympathised with their plight, backed them. He challenged Nehru about it personally and accused him of treating the Nagas much as Britain had colonised the Irish, but to no effect. Indira Gandhi was also in favour of her father's plans. Scott had then brought Phizo and his daughter to England in the hope of raising some support for their cause. Since Russell had been friendly with Nehru it occurred to Scott to approach him on behalf of the Nagas. Hence the tea party. Scott intended to try to get Russell to put his signature to a plea to Nehru on behalf of the Nagas.

That was the background. The situation does not fit

easily into any coherent structure. The geography, the politics, an atheist philosopher, an Anglican priest and a Naga chief all congregated in a remote house in north Wales. Indeed, there would seem to be rather a negation of structure. Even the function came to grief. Russell declined to sign Scott's plea for the separate identity of Nagaland. He was sympathetic but protested that his signature had become so devalued that it might soon be worthless. Unknown to Russell, his American secretary Ralph Schoenman had done much to ensure this. Scott knew of Schoenman's manipulation of Russell and had taken the precaution of telephoning Plas Penrhyn to ascertain that Schoenman would not be there that day. It was not till later that Russell himself realised how much he was being manipulated.

There seems to be some broad resemblance in the above between the life of Michael Scott and that of Simone Weil. In both cases we see a fracture of conventional structures and attempts to set up a new one. There is, for instance, the importance of religion and left-wing thinking, the socialism, the impassioned defence of the helpless and the deprived. Michael represented the interests of the deprived Herero tribe in Namibia year after year at the United Nations in New York, as Simone defended the workers in the Renault factory in Billancourt. Neither Michael nor Simone had much regard for convention; nor did they care a jot for how they looked or dressed. Both were tireless workers. Simone fought in the Spanish Civil War. Michael had suffered violence and imprisonment in South Africa and became a rear-gunner in the RAF in the Second World War, an unlikely job for a priest. He also learned to become a pilot. Both were invalided out – Simone from an anarchist battalion in Spain, Michael from the RAF. Both, in belief, were pacifist. In stark contrast to those belligerent armchair warriors who have never seen a shot fired, Michael was a leader in the Campaign for Nuclear Disarmament.

Michael died some twenty or more years ago. His funeral took place in St. Martin-in-the-Fields to the sound of African drums and a valedictory sermon by Trevor Huddlestone. Archbishop Tutu attended a memorial celebration to which my wife and I were invited. Michael Scott was a structure-breaker. That was his function. Sometimes the sound of a breaking structure is heard as a shout of 'Eureka'. More often the sound is scarcely heard at all. No paradigm is shifted, no belief strengthened or abandoned, nothing is changed, at least on the face of it. So it was with Simone Weil and Michael Scott. The world moves on, as it has always done, as if it had no ears.

A Reader's Guide

The reader is invited to question everything in the foregoing and no doubt will. The writer has tried to be undogmatic but one must necessarily have one's own personal point of view. The structures and patterns which have been features in various chapters should not be regarded as in any way inflexible or unalterable. They are merely vehicles for concepts and may associate as much as separate. There is a tendency in any enquiry to compartmentalise, to isolate a subject in pursuit of more penetrative observation. One of the objects of this book, however, is to break down barriers and cross frontiers, not only between disciplines but in the process of thought itself. It should not, for example, be unthinkable to think the unthinkable, and if this means considering the absurd, then so be it. The absurd has an absurd habit of appearing rational to future generations. Copernicus's discovery, relativity and quantum theory were once absurd.

It would seem a good idea, therefore, to consider a subject, a project or whatever from as many sides as one can. That time-saver 'Occam's razor' should not be universally applied (Entities should not be multiplied beyond what is necessary). Leave that to the reductionists. Who knows where what is necessary lies? Or even what it is? Many a new discovery has surely been cut short or delayed by William of Occam, that fourteenth-century Franciscan born near Guildford. Who knows what has been missed by scientists wielding his razor too enthusiastically?

It is suggested here that things should be considered from as many points of view as possible face-on, sideways, back view, athwart, upside-down, inside-out, centrally, peripherally, at the moment, in the past, in the possible future, its origin, its possible purpose, its form and content, its texture, its coherence or the lack of it. It should be assessed, where possible, appreciatively, critically, sensually and intellectually. Most important, of course, is its meaning. Never be content with the obvious, the orthodox or the authoritative. They are often a façade for obscuration, however stable and attractive they may appear. Life is an enigma, not a bare statement. In the writer's view we are here not to accept it at face value but to attempt to solve the riddle. In Goethe's words: 'Alles Vergängliche ist nur ein Gleichnis' (Everything transitory is but a metaphor).

There is also the question of language. It is an inadequate tool, a sieve for the riddling of fluid concepts, a structure which lets through as much as it retains. That great humanist Erasmus recommended in his 'Enchiridion' (Gk. a handbook or manual) that readers should not limit themselves to literal interpretation of texts but look beyond them for the original meaning, to the spirit rather than the letter. This seems, to the writer, especially relevant to science, where precision is seen as essential and 'facts' taken as indisputable. Scientific rigour may be necessary for manipulation, but not for understanding. For the latter one must often 'sit loosely to the text'.

Index